GLAD YOU ASKED!

ANSWERS TO 12 TOUGH QUESTIONS ABOUT CHRISTMAS THAT YOU NEED ANSWERS FOR

PRESENTED BY

reasons*for*hope*

Trilogy Christian Publishers

A Wholly Owned Subsidiary of Trinity Broadcasting Network

2442 Michelle Drive

Tustin, CA 92780

Copyright © 2023 by Reasons for Hope, Inc.

Unless otherwise indicated, Scripture quotations are taken from the ESV® Bible (The Holy Bible, English Standard Version®), copyright © 2001 by Crossway Bibles, a publishing ministry of Good News Publishers. Used by permission. All rights reserved.

Scripture quotations marked NKJV are taken from the New King James Version®. Copyright © 1982 by Thomas Nelson. Used by permission. All rights reserved.

All rights reserved, including the right to reproduce this book or portions thereof in any form whatsoever.

For information, address Trilogy Christian Publishing

Rights Department, 2442 Michelle Drive, Tustin, CA 92780.

Trilogy Christian Publishing/ TBN and colophon are trademarks of Trinity Broadcasting Network.

For information about special discounts for bulk purchases, please contact Trilogy Christian Publishing.

Trilogy Disclaimer: The views and content expressed in this book are those of the author and may not necessarily reflect the views and doctrine of Trilogy Christian Publishing or the Trinity Broadcasting Network.

10 9 8 7 6 5 4 3 2 1

Library of Congress Cataloging-in-Publication Data is available.

ISBN 979-9-89041-601-8

ISBN (ebook) 979-9-89041-602-5

ACKNOWLEDGMENTS

For over 20 years now, I've focused on reaching the younger generation with the truth of God's Word and sharing WHY Christians can trust the Bible in a culture gone crazy, and I do mean crazy. If you don't see what I'm talking about, please come to one of our EQUIP Retreats and interact with the youth the way we do. In my humble opinion, this generation is under attack more than any generation in the past.

Years ago, we started handing out index cards at our camps and asking attendees to write down and turn in the questions that keep them from selling out for the Lord Jesus Christ. Our speakers then work through those questions from a biblical perspective, showing that God's Word still applies to what we see in our world today. It never grows old!

This practice has led to us starting a series of question-and-answer books entitled *Glad You Asked!* because we're so very glad they asked us their questions instead of walking away from their faith dissatisfied that they didn't get answers to their questions. In the process of working through the issues these young people have raised, we help them to begin trusting the Scriptures.

A book like this doesn't just happen without A LOT of behind-the-scenes work. I have to say a HUGE "Thank You!" to Holly Varnum, who poured herself into this project. Juan Valdes did an amazing job of triple-checking to make sure we weren't falling off a cliff theologically. Hannah Dukes once again blessed us with her editing/proofreading skills. The kind folks at Trilogy Publishing, namely Mark Mingle and Rachel Hiatt, went way above and beyond to pull all the stops to get it out in a timely manner. Dan Lietha (I am so privileged to work with this unbelievably talented artist),

THANK YOU for your art that just makes things work. Andy Stearns from Faith Baptist Bible College (faith.edu), you bless us that you would take the time to help while working through health issues with your dear wife. David Madsen, professor at Maranatha Baptist University (mbu.edu), what a blessing to have you write one of these chapters for us. Authors from the Reasons for Hope team—Candace, Frank, Dave—you humble and bless me. Thank you for sharing your talents to help fulfill these crazy ideas I have.

Lastly, and most importantly, we pour our thanks out to our Lord and Savior, Jesus Christ. Why He allows me to do the things that I do are beyond me. His birth is so important, and we need to take a look at some of the issues addressed in these chapters that I believe make it difficult for some people to trust Him. Here's our humble offering, Lord Jesus. Please use it to bring many to a saving knowledge of Christ; that is my heart's desire.

Stay Bold!

ISA. 41:10-13

THE REAL REASON FOR OUR HOPE

The Bible teaches that God created everything and called His creation *very good.* He created man in His image, then He made a woman from the man, and the man, Adam, named her Eve. God gave them dominion over all creation, and He also gave them free choice (Genesis 1 & 2).

Man and woman were in perfect paradise, naked and unashamed, with only one restriction—they were commanded not to eat from a specific tree in the garden where God had placed them. God warned them that if they disobeyed Him, it would be sin, and death would follow (Genesis 2:17). Tempted by Satan through the form of a serpent, Eve ate from the forbidden tree and gave the fruit to Adam. He ate it, too. At that moment, mankind had sinned against God. A holy God must deal justly with sin, so He did (Genesis 3). Because man had dominion over all God created, the entire universe was cursed, meaning we all now live in a corrupt and fallen world full of death, suffering, pain, evil, tears, and toil. The sin nature had entered reality.

Since then, we have all sinned and fallen short of the glory of God (Romans 3:23), and the consequences are terrifying. Dead in our trespasses, we are all doomed to eternal destruction away from the presence of the Lord and from the glory of His might (Romans 6:23). There is nothing—not one thing—you or I can do to save ourselves. BUT HERE'S THE GOOD NEWS—here's the *GOSPEL*: God loves us so much that He sent His one and only Son to rescue us (John 3:16)—Jesus, Emmanuel, God with us—fully God and fully man, born of a virgin, conceived by the Holy Spirit.

Jesus lived a perfect and sinless life, which makes Him *uniquely qualified* to pay for our sins and rescue us from God's wrath. Not only did He step down into humanity, but He was executed on a cross in our place. He was pierced for our sins and crushed for our rebellion. Upon Him was our punishment, and by His wounds, we are healed (Isaiah 53:3–6). Amazing love … amazing grace. But that's not all. Jesus, after being placed in a tomb for three days, was resurrected, thus conquering the last enemy—death. So powerful is the work and name of Jesus that whoever believes in Him will not perish but have eternal life (1 John 4:9,10).

So wonderful is His mercy and grace that all who call upon His name, confess with their mouths, and believe in their hearts that He was raised from the dead shall be saved (Romans 10:9). And the one whom Jesus saves is no longer condemned (Romans 8:1) but is completely set free and will dwell in the unimaginable new heavens and new earth with Jesus and His co-heirs forever (Revelation 21:1–3).

There will be no more pain, no more sin, no more suffering, no more death, no more evil, and no more tears or toil. Why? Because Christ Himself will make all things new (Revelation 21:4,5). This is the full gospel and the most important message you'll ever hear.

To see and share this same message in animated video form, please scan the QR code here.

TABLE OF CONTENTS

FOREWORD

The arrival of the Christmas season is a special time filled with great anticipation. We look forward to the family get-togethers, special foods made only for this occasion, the exchange of gifts, the carols of the season, and those well-remembered Christmas programs put on by the Sunday School Department.

I remember well my varied roles in these programs, which included the prophet Micah who foretold the place of the Messiah's birth. I played the role of a shepherd who was first frightened by the angelic appearance, then made his way to the location of the Savior's birth. Most memorable was portraying the angel who made announcements to Mary, Joseph, and then to the shepherds. All this to describe what happened during this wonderful event, which brought light and hope to a world entrapped in darkness and despair.

While today's culture places emphasis on commercialism and all the secular trappings, as believers in Christ we recognize the significance of this event. *"And we have seen and do testify that the Father sent the Son to be the Savior of the world"* (I John 4:14). Indeed, the Promised One, the Messiah, had come!

Yet questions loom regarding the birth of Christ and whether or not it should be observed or celebrated. While we may be tempted to sweep certain matters under the rug, this book will provide answers to many key questions that surround this day. The multiple writers take a careful look examining the Scriptures to help you separate biblical truth from error on many important matters.

In hosting *Crosstalk*, a national daily talk show, there have been periodic callers who insist that believers in Christ should have nothing to do with Christmas or its observance. And yet, as I see the pages of Scripture unfold, I find that Mary rejoiced (Luke 1:46–47), the angels rejoiced (Luke 2:10–14), the shepherds rejoiced (Luke 2:17, 20), Simeon rejoiced (Luke 2:25–32) and Anna rejoiced (Luke 2:36–38) With all of these rejoicing and celebrating the birth of the Savior I find I'm in good company as I also rejoice!

Jim Schneider, Executive Director
VCY America Inc.

PART ONE

TRADITIONS: ARE YOURS BIBLICAL?

CHAPTER 1

IS CHRISTMAS A PAGAN HOLIDAY?

Andy Stearns

Imagine a Christian who walked into a room decorated with satanic pentagrams and paintings of Hindu deities. On the mantel are some traditional Aztec idols, and on the back wall is a large painting of Thor and Odin. Immediately, a shaman-type figure walks up to the believer and says, "Would you like to worship the all-father in our human sacrifice ritual?" What would a true believer do in a situation like that?

Leave.

There is no question about it. A believer knows that worship is reserved for God and God alone. But some have said that Christians are just as pagan as the shaman in the fictional story above. Why would someone say that? "Because, don't you know? Christmas is a pagan holiday." A claim like this could alarm a naïve Christian or one with a tender conscience. Fears of unwittingly being a part of a pagan worship ritual might even come to mind. Unwrapping presents? Using a Christmas tree? Singing songs? Celebrating near the winter solstice? Is Christmas *really* a pagan holiday?

To answer this question, we first need to clarify what we mean by "pagan." We will study two Roman holidays to see what pagan holidays look like. Then we will study the Christmas holiday. What was it like, and what is it celebrating? Finally, we will compare these different holidays and decide if Christmas is really a pagan holiday after all.

PAGAN HOLIDAYS IN ANCIENT ROME

Rome was filled with many different religious beliefs and, thus, many different religious celebrations. Two pagan festivals are worth looking at: *Saturnalia* and *Sol Invictus*. Both were celebrated in the Roman Empire after Jesus' resurrection, and both were celebrated around December 25.

SATURNALIA

Rome, borrowing Greece's pantheon of gods, worshiped the god Saturn (also known as Cronus). He was believed to be an agricultural god and was celebrated at the winter solstice when the harvest was finished. His festival, named *Saturnalia*, began as a single day and eventually stretched as long as a week. Most historians think the festival started around December 17, depending on the year. But for most of its history, the primary day of celebration was none other than December 25. What was the celebration like? Several festivities were wrapped up in *Saturnalia*.

- First, it was a time of partying and frivolity. Celebration and feasting were common.
- Second, it was a time to swap roles. Farmhands would be served by their landowners. Slaves would be served by their masters.

- Third, a general "good will toward men" sentiment prompted exchanging gifts.[1]

While celebrating and giving gifts might seem similar to Christmas, one significant difference needs to be pointed out. This was unlike any Christmas party you have had at your church or with your family. It was filled with debauchery, licentiousness, excessive drinking, and likely gambling. The poet Lucian of Samosata wrote a play with Saturn as one of its characters. When Saturn was asked about the celebration in his honor, this is how Lucian had him reply:

> Mine is a limited monarchy, you see. To begin with, it only lasts a week; that over, I am a private person, just a man in the street. Secondly, during my week, the serious is barred; no business allowed. Drinking and being drunk, noise and games and dice, appointing of kings and feasting of slaves, singing naked, clapping of tremulous hands, an occasional ducking of corked faces in icy water—such are the functions over which I preside.[2]

I've been to many Christmas parties. None have involved sexual immorality, drunkenness, or gambling. In fact, I can't think of any that involve those things, at least not Christmas parties that Christians plan and host. The description above sounds more like a kegger or a party at a frat house.

SOL INVICTUS

Sol Invictus was a religion that worshiped the sun (Sol). The history of the Solar Cult connects to the worship of the Syrian sun

---

[1] Fowler, *The Roman Festivals of the Period of the Republic*, 361–65.
[2] Samosata, *Works of Lucian of Samosata*, 611.

god, Baal.[3] The god Sol was also known as Mithra.[4] He and Sol are said to be "one god in two manifestations."[5] Emperor Aurelian, "an ardent worshiper of the Syrian sun god Baal"[6] made *Sol Invictus* the official imperial religion in AD 274.[7] The Romans believed Sol symbolized victory because he rose every morning, repeatedly showing his victory over darkness. Romans held chariot races in his name on December 25 each year, the day believed to be the birth of Sol. The celebration of *Dies Natalis Solis Invicti* ("Birth of the Unconquerable Sun") was devoted to the Sol/Mithra and involved exchanging gifts and making wishes.[8]

An interesting part of the history of this celebration was the later actions of Emperor Julian (AD 361-363). Constantine raised Christianity to central prominence (see below) following his edict in AD 313. Emperor Julian, who ruled about 30 years after his uncle Constantine, attempted to revive paganism in the empire. Julian was an opponent of Christianity. He "defied the Christianization that was the hallmark of his uncle's rule and issued edicts that favored Roman cults and minimized the influence of Christianity."[9] Julian made "the worship of Helios (the sun) the religious focus . . . of his efforts to revive paganism against Christianity."[10] However, the ill-fated "revival" would never happen.[11]

In light of this historical context, here's an important question: If Christmas were the same as *Sol Invictus*, why would Julian attempt to revive *Sol Invictus*? Why not just ride the coattails of the Christian revolution, as Rome had already done with the Greek

---

[3] Miles, *Christmas in Ritual and Tradition*, Christian and Pagan, 6.
[4] Clauss, *The Roman Cult of Mithras*, 146.
[5] Clauss, *The Roman Cult of Mithras*, 146.
[6] Miles, *Christmas in Ritual and Tradition*, Christian and Pagan, 6.
[7] Ferguson, *Backgrounds of Early Christianity*, 317.
[8] Jasiński, "Dies Natalis Solis Invicti « IMPERIUM ROMANUM."
[9] "Emperor Julian and the Dream of a Third Temple—The Jerusalem Post."
[10] Fowler, *The Roman Festivals of the Period of the Republic*, 6.
[11] Fowler, *The Roman Festivals of the Period of the Republic*, 6.

pantheon of gods? This clearly indicates that the two celebrations are not as similar as some might believe.

THE CHRISTMAS CELEBRATION: ORIGINS AND MEANING

Having looked at two pagan celebrations near Christmas, we now need to learn more about the Christmas celebration. Learning about its origin will help us to know if it came from pagan beliefs. Learning about its meaning and significance to Christians will show us whether Christians believe the same thing pagans believe about their holidays.

THE ORIGIN OF CHRISTMAS

In AD 312, a Roman emperor named Constantine converted from the pagan religion of *Sol Invictus* to follow Christianity. On the eve of a great battle at the Milvian Bridge, Constantine believed he had received a vision from Christ. This vision instructed him on how to win the battle. Constantine followed the instructions and won the battle. After this, he converted to Christianity. This was a shocking turn of events, and the effects would spread through the Roman Empire. Up to this point, Christianity existed as either a small religion or as a *persecuted* small religion. After the conversion of Constantine, it would soon become the dominant religion, because Constantine began to make changes that favored Christianity.

Constantine did not eradicate paganism. His empire was filled with pagans, so he had to be careful to appease them while he promoted (or at least privileged) Christianity. But he did emphasize Sundays, which "became one of the major days in the church calendar after Constantine decided that it was to be a day of civic

[rest] as well as religious worship."[12] Constantine also instituted the Christmas celebration.[13] The first celebration of Christmas took place near the year AD 350.[14] Cairns notes, "The festival of Christmas became a regular practice in the West about the middle of the fourth century, with the adoption of the December date that had been previously used by the pagans."[15] The date for Christmas was chosen because of its significance to the holidays of the pagan religions. But it was adopted only after it was "purged of its pagan elements."[16] In a sense, Constantine provided Christians a way to celebrate their God in opposition to the celebration of the pagan gods of Rome.

THE MEANING OF CHRISTMAS

Today, we see two types of Christmas celebrations. The commercialized version portrays Santa—a pudgy, gray-bearded man in a red suit and red hat—as a magical figure who brings presents to all the children on Christmas morning. He rewards good children with toys from their wish lists and punishes naughty children

[12] Cairns, *Christianity Through the Centuries*, 153.
[13] Shelley, "Is Christmas Pagan?," 85.
[14] Cairns, *Christianity Through the Centuries*, 153.
[15] Cairns, *Christianity Through the Centuries*, 153.
[16] Cairns, *Christianity Through the Centuries*, 116.

by giving them only a lump of coal.[17] But there is a second type of Christmas celebration as well. This is the true Christmas celebration. It focuses on the first advent of Christ and His nativity (birth).

Luke 2 details the events of Joseph and Mary, the census in Bethlehem, the birth of a baby in a manger, and the rejoicing of the hosts of heaven at this wondrous event. Christians sometimes celebrate both, though many ignore the fat man in the red suit.

One element of both Christmas celebrations is the Christmas tree. Christians set up a fir (or other evergreen) tree in their homes. They decorate it with lights and sparkly decorations. No matter what historic meanings you might see behind this tradition, you must reckon with the meaning Christians *today* give the Christmas tree.[18] The point is that Christians do not see themselves worshiping pagan deities when they set up a tree and put decorations on it.

[17] Please refer to Chapter 3, "Is Teaching Santa a Sin?" by Carl Kerby to learn more in-depth information about the origins of Santa Claus.
[18] See Chapter 2, "Is Having a Christmas Tree a Sinful Practice?" by Candace Nordine in this volume for a fuller treatment of this issue.

A significant element of the holiday is reading the Christmas story from Luke 2, usually on Christmas Eve or Christmas morning. However, this tradition isn't really part of the consumer Christmas holiday. Both groups do, however, exchange gifts with family during this season. But even then, Christians recognize that the birth of Jesus is the "reason for the season."

You can think of Christmas this way: a pagan Roman emperor converts to Christianity, then reacts against the pagan celebrations by creating a celebration of the Savior's birth. This celebration was not centered on drinking, partying, or anything associated with pagan religions. It was a time to rejoice that God had sent His Son to be the Savior of all the world. Is Christmas commanded anywhere in the Bible? Nope. You won't find that. Is the birth of the Son of God a good thing for Christians to celebrate in holiness and purity? Absolutely!

SO WHY WOULD SOMEONE SAY CHRISTMAS IS PAGAN?

The question remains: are these holidays all the same but with different names? Some would say, "Yes!" They would base it on the similarities they see. *Saturnalia* was celebrated on the same date as Christmas, December 25. It also involved the giving and exchanging of gifts. And its overall tone was that of general goodwill toward men. *Sol Invictus* was also celebrated on December 25 and involved gift-giving and general merriment.

But the differences are absolutely massive and far outweigh these similarities. Additionally, the differences occur at the level of *essential* characteristics and not merely *accidental* characteristics. No matter how many accidentals you might have in common, you must have the same essential characteristics to say that two objects are the same thing.[19] For example, a dog is a different animal than a cat. The *essential qualities* of both are different. But a dog and a cat might have the same color fur. This similarity is an *accidental* characteristic. No one would look at a black dog and a black cat and say they are the same animal.

Consider the following *essential* differences. First, the pagan holiday of *Saturnalia* included wicked acts (drunkenness, partying, etc.) that the Bible condemns. Christmas has nothing at all like that in its history. Remember Lucian's description from above? That sounds more like a kegger at a frat house than a celebration of the God who describes Himself as "holy, holy, holy" in the Bible (Isaiah 6:3; Revelation 4:8). In his book *The Battle for Christmas*, historian Stephen Nissenbaum recounts the "slave Christmas" in the American South. This was a phenomenon where the southern landowners would give their slaves a few days off around Christmas. Some of these slaves would take the opportunity and engage in "constant drinking and dancing," which evidently led to "intensified sexual activity."[20] When describing this celebration, some at the time called it "a modern version of the old Roman *Saturnalia*."[21] Stop and consider this point for just a moment. When people in the South saw partying involving drinking and debauchery, they did not call that "the normal Christian Christmas celebration."[22] Instead, they saw this as being the typical partying atmosphere of the Roman holiday of *Saturnalia*.

Second, pagan holidays celebrate, yep, you guessed it . . . pagan gods! Christians have never in their history believed they were worshiping Saturn or the Invincible Sun, just with a different name. Christians celebrate Jesus Christ, the Son of God, in the Christmas celebration.

---

[19] Oswalt makes a similar connection between the Bible and ancient myths. See Oswalt, *The Bible Among the Myths*, 13–14.
[20] Nissenbaum, *The Battle for Christmas*, 267.
[21] Nissenbaum, *The Battle for Christmas*, 267.
[22] Nissenbaum, *The Battle for Christmas*, 267.

Third, to worship any of these pagan gods is expressly condemned as idolatry. This is a fundamental difference between Christianity and these pagan religions. Christianity is monotheistic (mono=one, *theos*=god). The first of the Ten Commandments codifies this ("You shall have no other gods before me," Exodus 20:3). The Jewish *Shema* has been interpreted the same and adds the idea of being wholly devoted to the Lord as well (Deuteronomy 6:4). From Genesis to Revelation, you won't find any options to be a polytheist (poly=many, *theos*=god) in Christianity.

So, why would someone think Christmas is pagan? There are two reasons. First, some look only at the *accidental* similarities we have noted, assume an evolutionary or materialistic explanation, and conclude that Christmas is just another myth or religious observance that must have borrowed material from other religions. Second, some, seeing Constantine's purge of paganism when he set up Christmas as a Christian holiday, conclude that Christmas is just Constantine's religious creation. Again, this assumes that Christianity is *not actually true*, but just like the many pagan religious systems out there. Also, in Constantine's day, especially just after he legalized Christianity, many were likely adopting the emperor's new religion for status reasons. These didn't really believe in Christianity; they just followed the emperor. As such, they were not committed Christians but polytheists who merely wanted to satisfy the emperor so they could go about their lives as usual. But genuine believers have never syncretistically worshiped both pagan gods and the One True God during the Christmas celebration.

A FINAL CONSIDERATION: PRIDE MONTH OR PRAYER MONTH?

So, it appears that we are dealing with a genetic fallacy. That is where you attempt to show that two things are tied together because they have a distant connection. Think of your biological family. You are genetically connected to them, even if you believe in wildly different things. I know many families where the parents are Republicans, and the kids are Democrats. Or the kids are Christians, and the parents are atheists. Sure, you can say they are in the same family, but just because your parents are atheists or Republicans doesn't make you either of those. You have to really believe those things. Just because you are genetically connected to them doesn't make you the same thing regarding beliefs.

Perhaps this illustration will help. In 1999, President Bill Clinton declared that the month of June would be dedicated to the celebration of homosexuals and alternative lifestyles. "Pride Month" was born. It had been an important time in the LGBT community previous to this, but Clinton's official recognition marked a culture change in America. June would be dedicated to what they call "alternative lifestyles." These are all based on sinful behaviors that the Bible condemns. The LGBTQ+ movement calls this "Pride Month." You have likely seen the rainbow and transgender flags all over town in June. Big companies change their social media profiles to include rainbow flags and post content affirming these wicked lifestyles.

But recently, Christians have begun to ask why this month should be dedicated to sin. Instead, some have renamed the month in honor of Christian virtues. One person even suggested that Christians turn Pride Month into "Prayer Month" and pray daily for those caught up in homosexual sins.[23]

Now consider the following thought experiment. What if "Prayer Month" really took off in Christianity? And what if, 100 years from now, it became the third most celebrated Christian holiday after Christmas and Easter? Maybe Christians have "lunch prayer meetings" at their places of employment every Thursday of

[23] Matson, "Let's Turn Pride Month into Prayer Month."

the month. They may even include random acts of kindness each week as a central part of the holiday.[24] Consider how great that would be. A whole month is dedicated to praying for those caught up in sin and doing kind deeds to our neighbors. Wow! Talk about an excellent opportunity to share the gospel.

Now imagine someone takes issue with the practice and then claims that "Prayer Month is just a homosexual holiday." When asked why they think this, they reply, "Well, don't you know? It started as a month dedicated to homosexuality. Christians just copied it, and now it's a Christian version of that holiday." Let's be honest here, would you accept that claim? Would anyone accept that claim? No way. Not in a million years.

The two holidays might have started around the same time. The one might have even been an alternative for Christians. But no one honestly looking at the issue would say that Christians are wrong and just myth-believers because they have a holiday that competed with a wicked pagan holiday like Pride Month.

CONCLUSION: CHRISTMAS IS MOST CERTAINLY NOT A PAGAN HOLIDAY

No one could say that "Prayer Month" (if it were an actual Christian holiday) was a homosexual holiday because of the circumstances surrounding its beginning. In the same way, we just can't say Christmas is a pagan holiday based on the circumstances of when it began. They have different events and activities, with Christianity prohibiting the idolatry that the pagans practiced. Finally, the meaning of the holiday and the intent of the Christians who celebrate it in no way honor pagan gods. So, if someone tries

[24] This author is serious about this suggestion. Perhaps we should consider an entire month devoted to prayer and kind deeds.

to tell you Christianity is just another mythical, man-made, pagan religion, don't fall for it. Buy gifts. Put up a tree. Drink eggnog and kiss your spouse under the mistletoe. And then thank God for sending His Son to be the Savior of the world. You aren't being pagan. You're just "giving thanks in all things" and celebrating God for the "great things He has done."

CHAPTER 2

IS HAVING A CHRISTMAS TREE A SIN? WHAT ABOUT OTHER TRADITIONS WE TYPICALLY PRACTICE AT CHRISTMASTIME?

Candace Nordine

I'm not sure when it started, but for as long as I can remember, my family has done a time-lapse video of us decorating our Christmas tree each year. I know it was definitely before the age of smartphones, because we used to have to set up a tripod WITH A CAMERA and literally stop every few minutes, take a photograph, keep decorating, stop, take another photo, and … well, you get the picture. It also required video editing software to pull it all together. Thanks to smartphones, it's much easier in recent years. Now, we even have fun and try to make silly poses to be captured as part of the video. What takes us a few hours to do gets condensed into just a few minutes. It's such a fun memory to have and look back at those videos. Talking about this yearly family practice naturally opens the door to discussing our traditions. Are they sinful? Namely, is having a Christmas tree sinful?

First of all, where did the idea of having a Christmas tree come from? Was it a pagan practice? (Other chapters in this book talk about the origins of Christmas and other traditions, so I'll let you read about those elsewhere.) Still, regarding the Christmas tree specifically, MANY theories have been argued over—everything from Egyptian roots to the Garden of Eden and even German bakers. Regardless of the origin of the Christmas tree tradition, evergreens have been rooted in history for many cultures as a symbol of celebration, worship, and the afterlife.

> *The ancient Egyptians worshipped a god called Ra, who had the head of a hawk and wore the sun as a blazing disk in his crown. At the solstice, when Ra began to recover from his illness, the Egyptians filled their homes with green palm rushes, which symbolized for them the triumph of life over death.*
>
> *Early Romans marked the solstice with a feast called Saturnalia in honor of Saturn, the god of agriculture. The Romans knew that the solstice meant that soon, farms and orchards would be green and fruitful. To*

> *mark the occasion, they decorated their homes and temples with evergreen boughs.*
>
> *In Northern Europe, the mysterious Druids, the priests of the ancient Celts, also decorated their temples with evergreen boughs as a symbol of everlasting life. The fierce Vikings in Scandinavia thought that evergreens were the special plant of the sun god, Balder.*
>
> *Germany is credited with starting the Christmas tree tradition as we now know it in the 16th century when devout Christians brought decorated trees into their homes.*[25]

As I was growing up, my father was a church pastor in Northern Michigan. We always had a beautifully decorated giant Christmas tree in the front of our church, and every year he would tell a story about the Christmas tree and its origins, beginning with Martin Luther. While researching this chapter, I finally found the source of the story he would tell.[26] In 1959, a World Vision radio broadcast told how Luther brought an evergreen into his home. The story goes as follows:

> *So one day, he cut one down and brought it into the house, thinking to bring some of its beauty into his home to fight against the bleakness of the winter. He wanted it to stand there "evergreen" as a reminder to his children that when the world was at its bleakest moment—sad and helpless and covered with a weight of sin—God sent his Son, everlasting life itself, to bring hope in the midst of the dark and chill.*

---

[25] History.com Editors, "History of Christmas Trees," *History*, April 24, 2023.

[26] AA Christmas Trees, "The Complicated History of the Christmas Tree," *AA Christmas Trees*, September 21, 2021.

> *He explained to his children that the tree is green in the winter like our faith in Christ. It stays fresh even in a time of trouble. Our faith in Christ stays green even in sorrow. It stays alive even in the midst of despair.*
>
> *Then Martin Luther put candles on the tree, saying, "The candles remind us of the star that led Wise Men to the Christ child."*[27]

Personally, this symbolism tied to the Christmas tree is my favorite. Whether or not Martin Luther originated the idea of having a Christmas tree in a home, he made it God-honoring and chose to put God's glory on the forefront.

Secondly, if you know my writing, I always like to define the terms we are discussing . . . it just keeps things clear. If we want to know if having a Christmas tree is a sin, a good place to start is defining what sin is. Good ol' Merriam-Webster's dictionary defines sin as "an offense against religious or moral law, transgression of the law of God."[28] In the book of Exodus, God gives us the Ten Commandments to know the law—a definition of sorts as to what breaking His law looks like. We won't ever keep the law perfectly, so that's why Jesus came (Matthew 5:17–20), but He gave us a definition so we would know what honoring and glorifying God might look like.

Measuring our questions against the law will get us to the crux of the matter. We don't have to look much farther than the second commandment, "*You shall not make for yourself a carved image, or any likeness of anything that is in heaven above, or that is in the earth beneath, or that is in the water under the earth. You shall not bow down to them or serve them* (Exodus 20:4–5a)." Here we

---

[27] Marilee Pierce Dunker, "The Origins of Decorating the Christmas Tree," *World Vision*, November 30, 2018.
[28] Merriam-Webster.com Dictionary, s.v. "sin," accessed August 18, 2023.

should ask a fundamental question: Is having a Christmas tree or keeping Christmas traditions an idol?

People often refer to two Scripture passages when suggesting that Christmas trees are idols: Jeremiah 10:1–16 and Isaiah 44. Both passages discuss cutting down trees and fashioning them into forms people could bow down, worship, or pray to. The *Got Questions* website states plainly, "So unless we bow down before our Christmas tree, carve it into an idol, and pray to it, these passages cannot be applied to Christmas trees."[29]

However, there is another way to look at it. My pastor defines an idol as *"Anything or anyone that begins to capture your heart, mind, and affection more than God."* Regarding possessions or things (like a Christmas tree or tradition), I'm reminded of the passage in Luke 18 about Jesus and the rich young ruler (Luke 18:18–24).

> *And a ruler asked him, "Good Teacher, what must I do to inherit eternal life?" And Jesus said to him, "Why do you call me good? No one is good except God alone. You know the commandments: 'Do not commit adultery, Do not murder, Do not steal, Do not bear false witness, Honor your father and mother.'" And he said, "All these I have kept from my youth." When Jesus heard this, he said to him, "One thing you still lack. Sell all that you have and distribute to the poor, and you will have treasure in heaven; and come, follow me." But when he heard these things, he became very sad, for he was extremely rich. Jesus, seeing that he had become sad, said, "How difficult it is for those who have wealth to enter the kingdom of God!"*

You see, the rich young ruler couldn't give up the one thing that mattered most to him: wealth. It was his identity, security,

[29] "Should We Have a Christmas Tree?" *Got Questions Ministries.*

and sense of worth to which he looked for significance and purpose. So, when it comes to Christmas trees and Christmas traditions, how tightly are you holding on to them? Some questions you might ask yourself are:

- Can I "survive" Christmas without getting a Christmas tree?
- Am I so focused on presents and the next bestselling gift I want to give or receive that I'm not even thinking about Jesus?
- What am I spending my time and money on during Christmas?
- Do I get more excited about Santa than Jesus?

After you examine your heart, if any of these questions apply, having a Christmas tree and maintaining certain traditions might just be an idol in your life and, thus, a sin. You might need to repent and change how you celebrate Christmastime. Even if you could answer "no" to these questions, it is always worth considering and praying about before the Lord to keep yourself and your family on track with what glorifies God.

At the beginning of this chapter, I shared that my family puts up a Christmas tree every year (a live one, for that matter), and we, like so many of you, have various Christmas traditions. Is there then a way we can honor God AND keep our traditions?

It can be helpful to remember that traditions and celebrations are biblical. In the Old Testament, we see the Jews keeping the feasts of the Lord to help them remember God's faithfulness and rejoice in His blessings. In the New Testament, Jesus celebrates Passover before His death by feasting with His disciples at the "Last Supper" (Luke 22:14–20). Regardless of the time of year, it's always good to ask yourself the motives behind your traditions. Are they God-honoring? What is their focus?

In Scripture, we see the Pharisees getting trapped in their traditions while Jesus constantly tried to point them to His Father (Matthew 15:1–9).

> *Then Pharisees and scribes came to Jesus from Jerusalem and said, "Why do your disciples break the tradition of the elders? For they do not wash their hands when they eat." He answered them, "And why do you break the commandment of God for the sake of your tradition? For God commanded, 'Honor your father and your mother,' and, 'Whoever reviles father or mother must surely die.' But you say, 'If anyone tells his father or his mother, "What you would have gained from me is given to God," he need not honor his father.' So for the sake of your tradition you have made void the word of God. You hypocrites! Well did Isaiah prophesy of you, when he said: 'This people honors me with their lips, but their heart is far from me; in vain do they worship me, teaching as doctrines the commandments of men.'"*

I love how *Got Questions* summarizes this issue:

> Traditions, no matter how ancient they may be, only have value if they are grounded in God's truth and point us to Him. Tradition must be under the authority of God and His Word; any tradition that contradicts God's Word or distracts us from it should be discarded. Tradition may be how we practice our faith, but our faith is founded on God's truth, not fallible human tradition.[30]

[30] "What does the Bible Say About Traditionalism?" *Got Questions Ministries.*

In conclusion, looking deeper into this topic has caused me to reminisce. We've had more than one year when that Christmas tree time-lapse video didn't happen. One year, bugs hatched in our live tree. Another year our tree stand broke, and we almost flooded our carpeted flooring; in fact, we didn't have a Christmas tree at all after this mishap. Regardless, at Christmas, whether we get a Christmas tree or not, we get to prioritize celebrating the gift of Jesus Christ in ALL our traditions. We rejoice that He came down to earth to make atonement for us! Also, knowing Christ as our Savior means we no longer have to be separated from our holy, loving God—which is worth celebrating! "So, whether you eat or drink, or whatever you do, do all to the glory of God" (1 Corinthians 10:31).

CHAPTER 3

WHAT ARE SANTA'S ORIGINS? IS TEACHING SANTA A SIN?

Carl Kerby

Without a doubt, most of us are familiar with the Christmas song about "someone" who seems to know almost everything about us, especially when it comes to whether we're awake or not and how we've acted over the past year. In fact, during the Christmas season, we'll hear or even sing this song ourselves multiple times. And though it sounds as if we're actually referring to God, "Santa Claus Is Coming to Town" is about what is reportedly "the world's most popular non-biblical saint for centuries."[31] So far, I've found 25 names for this supposedly jolly old fellow, including the Hawaiian name "*Kanakaloka*."[32] Of course, you know who I'm speaking about, and it's the cultural icon, Father Christmas, or Santa Claus. As Christians, what are we to do with what has become probably the most commercial figure on our planet? Is teaching Santa a sin?

---

[31] Green Global Travel, "The Story of St. Nicholas," Point #5.
[32] Mary Puku'I, nd, "Kana Kaloka," *Huapala.org*.

In full disclosure, my wife and I both came to the Lord when our children were between the ages of four and six. Our perspective on this issue changed after this happened. Before salvation, we taught about Santa. After our conversion, we both felt we shouldn't intentionally mislead our children, even about Santa. We believed that if we did, when they found the truth out later, it would cause them to wonder what other things we may not have been entirely truthful with them about, including Jesus.

So, we told our children the truth but also taught them that they should respect other parents' desires regarding what they led their children to believe. They weren't to lie; they should simply avoid the conversation or use it as an opportunity to share about where "Santa" came from and how ultimately, "Jesus was the reason for the season." So, what are Santa's origins?

It depends on which Santa we're talking about!

Let's start by addressing the version created by the marketing machines here in America! In 1822, American writer Clement Clarke Moore was hosting a Christmas party at his home and read a poem he had written for his children as a Christmas gift.[33] That poem, "A Visit from St. Nicholas," began with:

[33] Paul Hond, "The Story Behind the Most Famous Christmas Poem of All," *Columbia Magazine*, November 19, 2021.

'Twas the night before Christmas when all through the house
Not a creature was stirring, not even a mouse.

It is doubtless that you know much of the rest of this poem—arguably the most well-known writing concerning Santa today. Later published in 1837, "'Twas the Night Before Christmas" is still as popular as ever. Moore's version of Santa was of a jolly, plump man with a white beard and twinkling eyes who smoked a pipe and delivered toys to children on Christmas Eve. This description is similar to what we see today in commercials trying to get us to buy anything from a car to a Coke©.[34]

Then there's the Santa that supposedly lives in the North Pole. This version of Santa is attributed to an image created by American artist Thomas Nast in 1866.[35] After the Civil War ended, Nast (who had drawn Santa previously) was tasked with creating a two-page spread for the publication *Harper's Weekly*. This artwork was entitled *"Santa Claus and His Works"* and contained many images that later became the foundation for what we currently see and

[34] Hond, "The Story," 2021.
[35] Patrick Young, Esq. (12/18/2017). "How German Refugee Thomas Nast Invented How Santa Claus Looks Back During the Civil War," *Long Island Wins*, December 18, 2017.

hear about Santa Claus. It was later published in color as a children's book and is still sold today.

There's also a man named St. Nicholas, who lived in what is now Turkey. He's also called "Nicholas of Bari" or "Nicholas of Myra."[36] Nicholas is believed to have been born around A.D. 280. He was reportedly well-known for his love and kindness to sailors, the poor, and children. There are many legends of his willingness to help those in need, with one of the most famous being that: *"He saved three poor sisters from being sold into slavery or prostitution by their father by providing them with a dowry so they could be married."*[37]

There aren't any verifiable historical documents that Nicholas ever truly existed, but there are many traditions concerning him. For example, he supposedly "*attended the first Council of Nicaea (A.D. 325), where he allegedly struck the heretic Arius in the face,*" leading to his imprisonment by Constantine the Great.[38] Please understand that I'm not advocating violence, but I would love to see more believers upset by the false teaching that perme-

[36] Editors of Encyclopedia Brittanica, nd,. "Santa Claus," *Britannica*.
[37] History.com Editors, "Santa Claus," *History*, April 20, 2023.
[38] The Archaeologist Editor Group, "Saint Nicholas of Myra: The Real Story Behind Santa Claus," *The Archaeologist*, December 6, 2021.

ates the Church today. December 6 was set aside and designated St. Nicholas Day to commemorate St. Nicholas and his kindness. It's still observed by many around the world. Starting on the fifth of December, children will put their shoes out with carrots and hay for St. Nicholas's horses, hoping he will exchange them for gifts.[39] Does this sound familiar?

Interestingly, the depiction of St. Nicholas has changed significantly over time. Early on, he wasn't the pleasant, happy fellow we see taking pictures with children in malls today. In Germany in 1850, he was referred to as Kris Kringle and was characterized as someone who *"appears to be on the verge of something violent. He needs professional help."*[40] Yes, he did deliver sweets and presents to good children, but he also gave lumps of coal, potatoes, or switches to bad ones.[41] I'm glad that wasn't the Santa Claus I grew up hearing about because I'm afraid we would've had many switches in my house since I was such a knucklehead! So, which of these three should we remember or celebrate? The answer to that is easy: none of them.

Though the history surrounding St. Nicholas is fascinating (and I've just scratched the surface with what I've shared here), I'd highly encourage you to research with your children and see what other legends you can dig up. However, I'll warn you that some portrayals are not so good, and some are downright scary, e.g., the story about "The Evil Butcher."[42] (I'm not sure I'd want most children to see that one, so be careful.)

The truth is that Santa Claus has become an integral part of Christmas celebrations. Because of this fact, I believe it's vitally

---

[39] Catherine Boeckmann, "St. Nicholas Day Traditions, History, and More," *Almanac*, May 24, 2023.
[40] Jim Hillibish, "The Evolution of Santa: From Nasty to Nice and Everything in Between," *The State Journal-Register*, December 21, 2008.
[41] The Editors of Encyclopaedia *Britannica*, "St. Nicholas Day," *Britannica*, July 28, 2023.
[42] St. Nicholas Center, nd, "The Evil Butcher," *St. Nicholas Center*.

important for Christians to remember the proper focus of Christmas. It isn't with a plump, jolly man riding around the earth in a sled pulled by reindeer but in the birth of our Lord and Savior, Jesus Christ. The celebration of Christmas should revolve around the acknowledgment and remembrance of Christ's coming into the world as the ultimate gift of salvation, available to all.

To the culture, Santa Claus represents generosity, kindness, and the joy of giving. From a Christian perspective, these are virtues worth celebrating. We can approach the idea of Santa Claus with others as a picture of the spirit of selflessness and love.

I believe we must emphasize that Santa Claus is a fictional character and not a substitute for the true meaning of Christmas. We must teach WHY the attributes of generosity, kindness, and the joy of giving are so important in a world gone crazy.

For the next generation to understand WHY Christians believe these attributes to be vitally important, we must teach them where the foundation and justification for those attributes come from. They are not important because I, you, or anybody else think they are. They're important because they align with the teachings and actions of a real man named Jesus Christ, who was fully God and fully man. He is the one who truly exemplifies the following: His death, burial, and resurrection are the "stamp" that He was who He claimed to be—God incarnate! If our children don't know WHY we believe what we believe, they can be easily persuaded to turn from the truth towards a lie.[43]

Jesus' death, burial, and resurrection are of utmost importance, but so too is His birth. The fact that Jesus was born of a virgin, as prophesied hundreds of years in advance in Isaiah 7:11–16 is an

---

[43] Please consider using Dr. Juan Valdes' book, *How to Think* to teach your children critical thinking skills. Also, watch our powerful DeBunked video, It Doesn't Matter Why You Believe . . . DeBunked! All of our DeBunked series videos are available on our free App—search for "rforh" on your App Store, Roku, or Apple TV.

excellent example of the trustworthiness of the Bible. It points to divine authorship, since no human would have ever been able to predict such a peculiar event. It gives us great hope that we can believe what we are taught throughout the rest of the Bible (see also chapter 9 on this topic).

Our loving Savior, Jesus Christ, knows we've all been "bad" (Romans 3:23); for that, we deserve to be separated from Him for all eternity.[44] But, even when we were bad and rejected Him, God gave us the greatest gift that could ever be given: He sent His only begotten Son to this earth to save us from our sins (Matthew 1:23). He's called Immanuel which literally means "God with us" (Matthew 1:22–23.) He is the true example of selflessness and love, and that's because while we were yet sinners, He loved us so much that He died for us (Romans 5:8).

I'd like to offer you the best Christmas gift you could ever receive. No, the best gift ever… period! That is the free gift of eternal life by simply believing on the Lord Jesus Christ today (Acts 16:31). Right now! Wherever you are, you can do this. Simply humble yourself and pray to God. He hears your prayers. It doesn't matter what you've done or what's been done to you. What matters is what He did for you!

So, is it a sin to celebrate Christmas? If you take Christ out of it, yes. You can use this season effectively to teach about the most crucial decision any of us will ever make and pray we will all rejoice and remember what Christmas truly represents. Just don't use a Christmas tree to do it![45]

To summarize this idea, I'd like to share what Jim Schneider, Executive Director of *VCY America Inc.,* and a friend I greatly

---

[44] For more information on this topic, please refer to, "Is Hell Really Forever?" by Bub Kuns in Volume 1 *Glad You Asked! Answers to 28 Tough Questions Teens Are Asking About God and the Bible (that adults need to know, too).*
[45] I'm joking! Please read Candace Nordine's chapter, "Is Having a Christmas Tree a Sinful Practice?" about this and other common traditions.

respect, has stated on air: *"Since the angels rejoiced at the birth of Christ and the shepherds rejoiced at the birth of Christ, so also can we!"* Amen and . . . Stay Bold!

CHAPTER 4

WHY DON'T JEHOVAH'S WITNESSES CELEBRATE CHRISTMAS?

Candace Nordine

Jehovah's Witnesses (JW): those "Christians" that come knocking at your door hoping to share about their religion and why you should be part of it. If you haven't had a Jehovah's Witness come to your door, you probably haven't lived long enough, but wait; they will come. Or, if you're like me, you may have even seen them with a table of materials at a county fair or on a California boardwalk. Despite having their own version of the Bible (the New World Translation) and additional revelations or prophecies, Jehovah's Witnesses themselves will claim they are Christians. So, shouldn't these "Christians" want to celebrate Christmas? Well, they give four main reasons why they do not celebrate Christmas[46], which answers this chapter's question, but we will examine each of their four reasons and how they align with both Scripture and their own teachings.

One last thing before we dive in. If you are a JW reading this, please know I don't write about any of this to mock you. I write

[46] Watchtower Bible and Tract Society of Pennsylvania, nd, "Why Don't Jehovah's Witnesses Celebrate Christmas?" *JW.ORG*.

out of my deep love and care for you to know the truth because, as Jesus says in John 8:32, "the truth will set you free."

1. *Jesus commanded that we commemorate his death, not his birth.*—Luke 22:19, 20.

   The reference that JW refers to in Luke 22 is the *Last Supper,* when Jesus, with His disciples, commemorates what is to come: His death and, ultimately, His resurrection. Jesus Himself said, "Do this in remembrance of Me," and His death should be remembered, but Scripture NEVER says NOT to commemorate His birth.

   The Bible gives us extensive details about Jesus' birth. In all four Gospels, Matthew, Mark, Luke, and John, there are details or references to Jesus coming into this world and the purpose for which He came. "I came that they may have life and have it abundantly" (John 10:10).

   In Luke, we see a group of shepherds so excited about Jesus' birth that they went and spread the news far and wide (Luke 2:16–17). Far more impressive than that, we see a host (a multitude) of angels worshiping and praising God for the birth of Jesus (Luke 2:14). It really does sound like a party and something to be celebrated!

   Glory to God in the highest heaven,
   and on earth peace to those on whom his favor rests.

   Part of the issue is that JW don't believe Jesus is God in the flesh; they believe Him to be the archangel, Michael.[47] So, it is difficult to celebrate something as important as God coming in the flesh to save us from our sins when that's not what they believe.

[47] Watchtower Bible and Tract Society of Pennsylvania, nd, "Who Is the Archangel Michael?" *JW.ORG.*

2. *Jesus' apostles and early disciples did not celebrate Christmas. The New Catholic Encyclopedia says that "the Nativity feast was instituted no earlier than 243 [C.E.]," more than a century after the last of the apostles died.*

   My friend, Dr. Juan Valdes, would call this argument a logical fallacy (well, probably all of these arguments, actually). In fact, he's got a great critical thinking book called *How to Think* that you should check out.[48] I've definitely learned a lot from his insights.

   The Bible does not tell us if the apostles celebrated Christmas. It doesn't say they did. It doesn't say they didn't. Maybe they didn't throw baby showers or visit Hawaii either. The Bible does not tell us about the apostles celebrating wedding anniversaries, but we do, and so do JW. Just because the apostles didn't engage in certain celebrations does not mean we shouldn't. I could ask a JW, "Did the apostles have field service, shave their beards, build Kingdom Halls, or have a large printing facility?[49]" These are all things they currently practice or participate in as part of their religion. Did the apostles have more than the Bible itself to share the gospel? Because, again, the JW do. The answer to each of these questions would be "no."

   In reality, the apostles didn't do many things that we do today. They didn't drive cars, eat fast food, or use high-speed internet. According to this line of reasoning used by the JW, if the apostles didn't do these things, then we shouldn't either. Do you see the over-arching flaw in this argument?

---

[48] To learn more about this critical thinking resource, *How to Think*, and to order one for yourself, please go to store.rforh.com, and click on Books.
[49] Surviving Paradise Podcast, "Why Don't Jehovah's Witnesses Celebrate Christmas?" *YouTube.com*, December 26, 2022.

However, we do know the apostles participated in celebrations. They celebrated Passover and other biblical festivals that were customary to them. The bottom line is this: if something gives glory to God, it's worth celebrating.

3. *There is no proof that Jesus was born on December 25; his birth date is not recorded in the Bible.*

This argument is somewhat ironic for JW since they recognize multiple historical or important dates that aren't in the Bible either. Here are just SOME of the dates they recognize, also NOT in the Bible[50]:

» The Last Days began in 1799 (The Harp of God, 1928 ed., pp. 235–36, 239).

» Jesus started being present with His people in 1874, and He started ruling in heaven in 1878 (ibid., pp. 236, 239–40).

» The times of the Gentiles would end in 1914, resulting in the end of Armageddon, the fall of false religion, the end of all earthly governments, the

[50] Got Questions Ministries, nd, "What are the Jehovah's Witnesses' beliefs about Jesus' return in 1914?" *GotQuestions.Org*.

heavenly and earthly resurrections, and paradise on earth (Watchtower, July 15, 1894, p. 226)

» Jehovah's Witnesses believe that Christ Jesus had to wait until October 1914 before all authority was given to Him, and it was at that time that He became the King of God's heavenly kingdom.

I could go on and on, but to avoid making this chapter a book in and of itself, I'll stop.

Another irony is that before 1928, JW did, in fact, celebrate Christmas. Their own literature documents this practice.[51]

> *EVEN though Christmas day is not the real anniversary of our Lord's birth, but more properly the annunciation day or the date of his human begetting (Luke 1:28), nevertheless, since the celebration of our Lord's birth is not a matter of divine appointment or injunction, but merely a tribute of respect to him,* ***it is not necessary for us to quibble particularly about the date****. We may as well join with the civilized world in celebrating the grand event on the day which the majority celebrate—"Christmas day." (The Zion's Watchtower of 1904, p. 364).*

Even in a publication in 1921, there was an ad in the *Golden Age Magazine* for JW to earn extra Christmas money by selling "Miracle Oil."[52]

---

[51] Watchtower Bible and Tract Society, 1904 *Zion's Watch Tower.*

[52] Watchtower Bible and Tract Society, 1921 *The Golden Age Magazine.*

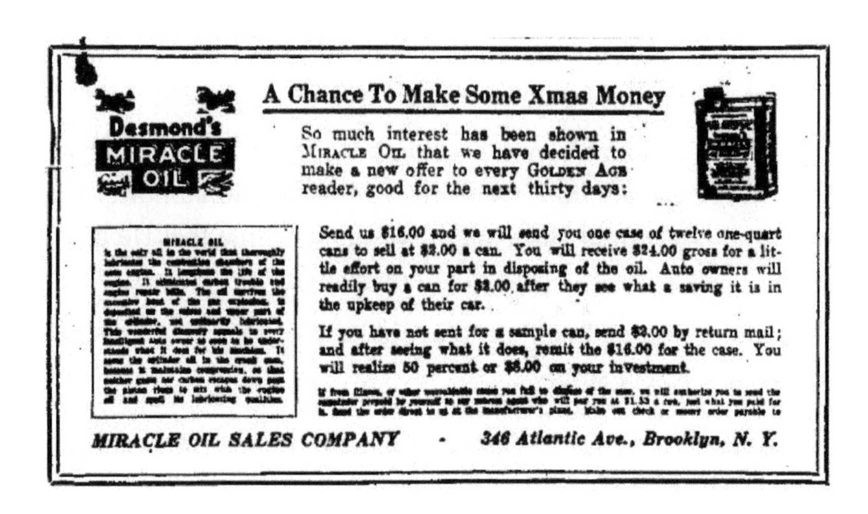

So what changed? In 1927, the JW "Bible students" came to believe that Christmas was a pagan holiday (Chapter 1, "addresses that issue.).

> *As a result of careful, closer scrutiny of the subject, the Bible Students came to realize that the origin of Christmas and the practices associated with it actually dishonor God. The article "The Origin of Christmas," in The Golden Age of December 14, 1927, noted that Christmas is a pagan celebration, focuses on pleasures, and involves idol worship. The article made it clear that the celebration was not ordered by Christ and concluded with this pointed statement about Christmas: "The fact that the world, the flesh, and the Devil are in favor of its perpetuation and observance . . . is a final and conclusive argument against its celebration by those who are dedicated wholly to the service of Jehovah." Not surprisingly, the Bethel family did not celebrate Christmas that December—or ever again!*[53]

[53] Watchtower Bible and Tract Society, nd, "The King Refines His People Spiritually" *JW.ORG*. 9

The truth is, we don't know what day Jesus was born . . . in fact, a chapter in this book deals with this very question, so be sure to read it (wink wink).[54] However, if God felt it essential for us to know the exact date, He certainly would have told us in His Word.

4. *We believe that Christmas is not approved by God because it is rooted in pagan customs and rites (2 Corinthians 6:17).*

   First, let's look into the context of the verse JW references here. I will include their New World Translation, as well as the wording of the ESV version.

   Therefore, get out from among them, and separate yourselves,' says Jehovah, 'and quit touching the unclean thing' and I will take you in. (NWT)

   Therefore go out from their midst, and be separate from them, says the Lord, and touch no unclean thing; then I will welcome you. (ESV)

To understand this verse better, we need a little bit of context. *Got Questions* explains it this way[55]:

> Paul quotes this passage from Isaiah in reference to the Corinthian church. He is taking familiar wording and giving it meaning in a fresh context. Just as the Israelites in exile were to put off any idolatry they may have picked up while living in Egypt, so the Corinthian believers are to lay aside the idolatry and sexual immorality that they were steeped in by virtue of living in Corinth. They must be separate from the sin of the world.

[54] Please refer to Chapter 8, "Was Jesus Actually Born on December 25th?" by Frank Figueroa, Jr.

[55]Got Questions Ministries, nd, What Does It Mean to Come Out From Among Them? *GotQuestions.org*.l

> Though addressing the church in Corinth, Paul's warning here about idolatry applies to all Christians.

Concerning Christmas, if instead, JW said, "We don't celebrate Christmas because we don't want it to be a stumbling block for the sin of idolatry," it would make more sense. However, they say they don't celebrate Christmas because it has pagan roots. My question to the JW is, "Where do you draw the line?" Wedding rings, wedding flowers, and even wedding anniversary celebrations have pagan roots. JW men are clean-shaven, but even that custom can have pagan roots. Pagans eat, sleep, and drink water, so should we also abstain from these "pagan rituals"? Using the same logic used to condemn Christmas, every JW who practices these things could be considered a pagan.

That's why Paul tells us in Romans 3:10, "There is no one righteous, not even one." Then later in chapter 3, he tells us what Jesus did for us despite all of us falling short, "for **all** have sinned and fall short of the glory of God, and are justified by his grace as a gift, through the redemption that is in Christ Jesus, whom God put forward as a propitiation by his blood, to be received by faith" (Romans 3:23–25). According to God's Word, without Christ, we are all "pagan." So despite our sinful flesh–Jesus, God in the flesh, came to earth to die for you and me to have secure hope. If we put our faith and trust in Him and Him alone, we can be saved and spend all eternity with Him.

In conclusion, after reading this chapter, I hope you know why JW don't celebrate Christmas, but more importantly, I hope that you see their reasoning is flawed because it is based on man-made teachings and not God's Word. True Christians may come to your door to share the gospel out of overwhelming love or compassion for you. Unfortunately, because of their belief system, JW are instead coming because they can only achieve "paradise on earth" by being faithful slaves of the *Watchtower*.[56] I hope this grieves you and compels you to share the gospel the next time a JW comes knocking at your door. I'll leave these words with you from my dear cousin, Jason Carlson, who has years of studying and speaking on different religions with Christian Ministries International.[57]

> *My father, Dr. Ron Carlson, used to remind people every chance that he could that the cults are literally a mission field at our front doorstep. Unfortunately, many Christians miss this tremendous opportunity to share our faith when the cultists, such as Jehovah's Witnesses or Mormons, come calling. For some people, taking the time to engage the cultist in a conversation is just too great an inconvenience. For others, the fear of not knowing what to say to the cultist at the door is justification enough for the common Christian response of, "No thank you, I'm a Baptist (or insert your particular denomination)."*
>
> *The sad reality, however, is that when we fail to engage the cultist in a conversation about spiritual truths, or at the very least share our personal testimony with them, we are neglecting a ready-made opportunity to minister to a lost soul who desperately needs to know the Lord. And the fact of the matter is this; you may be that cultist's last, best opportunity to hear the truth of the Gospel.*
>
> *This is why we must answer the door when the cultists come knocking. The eternal destinies of lost people are at stake. These are people God loves and whom He deeply desires to see come to repentance. And as I said earlier, we must never discount the possibility that we may be that cultist's last, best opportunity to hear the truth of the Gospel of Jesus Christ.*

---

[56] Ron Carlson, nd, "What Do Jehovah's Witnesses Believe?" *Christian Ministries International.*
[57] Jason Carlson, nd, "Why we Answer the Door When the Cultists Come Knocking," *ChristianMinistriesIntl.org.*

Remember, as Christians we are not responsible for how a person responds to our proclamation of the Gospel. We're simply responsible for being faithful with the opportunities we have to proclaim it. The next time the cultists come to your front door, please take a few minutes to share the truth of the Good News of Jesus Christ with them. They are literally a mission field at our front doorstep

PART TWO

CHRIST-MYTH BUSTERS

CHAPTER 5

DID JESUS REALLY HAVE THREE WISE MEN VISIT HIM AS A BABY? WHY DID THE MAGI BRING HIM GOLD, FRANKINCENSE, AND MYRRH? WHAT WAS THE "MASSACRE OF THE INNOCENTS"?

Frank Figueroa, Jr.

If you have ever looked at a Nativity scene, you have probably noticed a few things. First, there is usually a hay-filled stable with a manger in it, and Jesus is usually placed lying in the manger. Next, you have Joseph and Mary flanking Jesus, usually one on each side, with a look of parental care that only those who have just had a newborn would have. Then, you have many animals on the scene. After all, why wouldn't there be animals crowded around these strange people within their shelter? A few shepherds are scattered outside the stable and looking in with amazement. Lastly, one other group is usually there. The three wise men, or magi (and the camels they rode in on), each with a box in their hands containing one of the three gifts offered to Jesus: gold, frankincense, and myrrh.

We even have Christmas songs that portray this scene . . .

We three kings of Orient are
bearing gifts we traverse afar,
field and fountain, moor and mountain,
following yonder star.[58]

But how much of this scene is true? How many of these facts are actually biblical and not just a distorted representation based on assumption and tradition? Let's tackle one of them here . . . Did the wise men, or magi, actually visit Jesus in the stable while He was in the manger, and what gifts did they bring, if any?

Like we always should, let's start with what the Bible declares. In Matthew's second chapter, he unfolds the most comprehensive view of this account recorded for us in Scripture:

[58] From the original Christmas hymn written in 1857 by John Henry Hopkins, Jr.

Matthew 2:1–12

Now after Jesus was born in Bethlehem of Judea in the days of Herod the king, behold, wise men from the East came to Jerusalem, saying, "Where is He who has been born King of the Jews? For we have seen His star in the East and have come to worship Him." When Herod the king heard this, he was troubled, and all Jerusalem with him. And when he had gathered all the chief priests and scribes of the people together, he inquired of them where the Christ was to be born. So, they said to him, "In Bethlehem of Judea, for thus it is written by the prophet: 'But you, Bethlehem, in the land of Judah, Are not the least among the rulers of Judah; For out of you shall come a Ruler Who will shepherd My people Israel.' " Then Herod, when he had secretly called the wise men, determined from them what time the star appeared. And he sent them to Bethlehem and said, "Go and search carefully for the young Child, and when you have found Him, bring back word to me, that I may come and worship Him also." When they heard the king, they departed; and behold, the star which they had seen in the East went before them, till it came and stood over where the young Child was. When they saw the star, they rejoiced with exceedingly great joy. And when they had come into the house, they saw the young Child with Mary His mother, and fell down and worshiped Him. And when they had opened their treasures, they presented gifts to Him: gold, frankincense, and myrrh. Then, being divinely warned in a dream that they should not return to Herod, they departed for their own country another way.

Let's dispel some of the myths right away. First, the Bible does not say any "kings" or camels were a part of this story whatsoever. Depending on which Bible version we are reading, those who made the trip westward from the orient to Jerusalem are variously called "magi," or "wise men," not kings.

Second, we have no idea how many wise men there were. Because they are defined in the plural, there had to be more than one of them. But there is absolutely no record indicating how many there were. The reason many assume that there were three wise men is that they gave three gifts. (We'll get to what those gifts were and what they represented in a little bit.) But we have to ask ourselves, could there have only been two wise men and one gave two gifts and the other gave one gift? Or, could there have been 17 wise men and a few gave gifts, and the others gave nothing? The text certainly allows for this. We do not know how they traveled, either. Many traditions have them traveling by riding camels, which could be. But we have no solid evidence indicating any camels were present for the journey or when they met Jesus.

What we do know is that as soon as they arrived in Jerusalem, they were intercepted by Herod. Since Herod was not Jewish, but Idumean (Edomite), he married Mariamne, an heiress to the Jewish Hasmonean house, in order to make himself more acceptable to the Jews he now ruled. He was quite a clever warrior and orator, but he was also a shrewd diplomat. Because of these characteristics, he was absolutely cruel and merciless. This led him to be incredibly jealous and made him suspicious of anyone who might be after his position and power.

Since the magi were out and about and asking where Jesus "King of the Jews" was, Herod eventually got wind of this and needed to stop this threat in its tracks. After all, any mention of another possible "king of the Jews" threatened his prominence and filled him with inner rage. In fact, not only was Herod bothered, but according to Matthew 2:3, "all of Jerusalem" was bothered by him because he was starting to agitate the city due to his jealousy. But he had to control himself in order for his plan to exterminate the other king to work.

Playing it cool, Herod called the chief priests and scribes together for a meeting so they could brainstorm to find Jesus. They shared with him the prophecy contained in Micah 5:2, "But you, Bethlehem Ephrathah, though you are little among the thousands of Judah, yet out of you shall come forth to Me the One to be Ruler in Israel, whose goings forth are from of old, from everlasting." After Herod received this information, he secretly called the magi and asked them what time the star had appeared. Notice his concern was for the time of the star's appearance, not its meaning or significance.

He then instructs the magi to go on their way and let him know when they find Jesus so that he can worship Him too. But, since Herod was a liar and a hypocrite, God would later reveal to the magi that they were not allowed to let Herod know anything.

All of a sudden, the star reappears to the magi and leads them to Jesus by moving in the direction that they were to go. But notice what Luke 2:11 says, "And when they had come into the house, they saw the young Child with Mary His mother, and fell down and worshiped Him. And when they had opened their treasures, they presented gifts to Him: gold, frankincense, and myrrh."

The first thing that should strike us is that they came to a house. This was not a stable or a manger. There was no mention of animals around Jesus. Why? Because it was the shepherds, not the magi, who saw Jesus as a baby lying in a manger as stated in Luke 2:15–16:

> *So it was, when the angels had gone away from them into heaven, that the shepherds said to one another,*

> *"Let us now go to Bethlehem and see this thing that has come to pass, which the Lord has made known to us." And they came with haste and found Mary and Joseph, and the Babe lying in a manger."*

But notice that the wise men did not show up until Jesus was at a house and that at that point, Matthew 2:11 refers to Him as a "young child." This is huge in answering the questions that we asked in the beginning of this chapter. Why? If Jesus was already a young boy, He had to have been circumcised and Mary would have completed her time of purification. So why is that important? At the time that Mary and Joseph had to offer the sacrifice required for having a baby, they offered a pair of turtle doves:

Luke 2:22–24

> *Now when the days of her purification according to the law of Moses were completed, they brought Him to Jerusalem to present Him to the Lord (as it is written in the law of the Lord, "Every male who opens the womb shall be called holy to the LORD"), and to offer a sacrifice according to what is said in the law of the Lord, "A pair of turtledoves or two young pigeons."*

This was not the typical sacrifice, as Leviticus 12:6-8 makes it clear that a sacrificial lamb was required. But there was a provision made that if the couple was really poor, they could offer a pair of pigeons or turtledoves because they cost significantly less. This is where a key point on our timing comes into play . . . If they had received the gift of gold from the wise men while Jesus was lying in the manger, they would have had no problem affording the lamb required for the sacrifice. But Joseph and Mary didn't receive the gold and other gifts until much later when Jesus was already a young child and living in a house. Well, how old was He?

There is no way to be dogmatic on this point, but I would argue that He was probably close to two years old or slightly under that. How did I come up with that? Because that is the age that Herod capped his massacre of the innocent when he gave the decree to kill all the male children:

Matthew 2:16

> *Then Herod, when he saw that he was deceived by the wise men, was exceedingly angry; and he sent forth and put to death all the male children who were in Bethlehem and in all its districts, from two years old and under, according to the time which he had determined from the wise men.*

Because of all of these clarifications, we can see pretty definitively that the wise men did not visit Jesus as He was lying in the manger, but rather visited Him when He was a young child in a house. We do not know how the magi traveled. Nor do we know how many wise men there were, except that there had to be at least two or more because they were mentioned in the plural. But let's not forget the most important part of this narrative . . . When the wise men encountered Jesus, they worshipped Him!

The word "worship" in the Greek is *proskyneoœ,* meaning "to adore and bow oneself in adoration." This expresses the idea of falling down, prostrating oneself, and kissing the feet or the hem of the garment of the one honored. And this led them to give gifts. Their giving was not so much an addition to their worship, but rather it was an expression of their worship given from their overflowing and grateful hearts.

Let's look at the significance of their gifts.

- Gold was a symbol of nobility and royalty. (Genesis 41:4; 1 Kings 10:1–13). Matthew continually presents Christ as the King, and here we see the King of the Jews, the King of kings, appropriately being presented with royal gifts of gold.

- Frankincense was a symbol of Jesus' deity. It was a costly, beautiful-smelling incense that was used only for the most special of occasions. It was used in the grain offerings at the Tabernacle and Temple (Leviticus 2:2–16), and in certain royal processions (Song of Solomon 3:6–7), and sometimes at weddings if it could be afforded.
- Myrrh was a symbol of Jesus' beautiful humanity. It was also a perfume, not quite so expensive as frankincense, but nevertheless valuable. Some scholars suggest that myrrh represents the gift for a mortal, emphasizing Jesus' humanity. When it was mixed with other spices, it was used in preparation of bodies for burial, even Jesus' body (John 19:39).

In short, the wise men recognized Jesus as the King of Kings, as God Himself, who had come in human form and was ultimately going to give His life as a sacrifice for our sins.

Have we recognized this same Jesus? Do we visit with Him and worship Him regularly? Have we recognized the fact that He is royalty and is He sitting on the throne of our lives? Do we comprehend His Deity and that God Himself has come and dwelt among us? Have we come to grips with His humanity and truly understand that He bore a body of flesh with the ultimate purpose of dying for us? In short, have we received the gift of Jesus? If not, why not?

CHAPTER 6

IS JESUS' BIRTH STORY BASED ON A MYTH OR A RIP-OFF OF HORUS, MITHRAS, AND OTHER EGYPTIAN GODS?

Carl Kerby

This title question is based on a claim that seems to pop up yearly, especially around Christmas. In his "mockumentary" *Religulous*, Bill Maher interviewed Michael Job, an actor who portrayed Jesus at "The Holy Land Experience" (formerly in Florida), and said the following:

Bill Maher:	But the Jesus story wasn't original.
Michael Job:	How so?
Bill Maher:	Written in 1280 B.C., the Book of the Dead describes a god, Horus. Horus is the son of the god Osiris, born to a virgin mother. He was baptized in a river by Anup the Baptizer, who was later beheaded. Like Jesus, Horus was tempted while alone in the desert,

> healed the sick and the blind, cast out demons, and walked on water. He raised Asar from the dead. "Asar" translates to "Lazarus." Oh, yeah, he also had twelve disciples. Yes, Horus was crucified first, and after three days, two women announced Horus, the savior of humanity had been resurrected.[59]

So, is that claim valid? Did Jesus rip off Horus, Mithras, and other Egyptian gods? The short answer is . . . No! (Aren't you happy? That was easy; this is the shortest chapter in this book.) I assume you're not happy with a simple "no," so I'll flesh it out a bit more. Did Jesus rip off Horus? My question in return is, "Which Horus?" Horus the Elder, Horus the Younger, or Horus of Behdet (Edifu)?

Typically, when this claim is made, it refers to either Horus the Elder (HE) or Horus the Younger (HY). Because of that, we'll leave the Behdet/Edifu version out. Let's now compare Bill Maher's claims from above with the facts:

BORN TO A VIRGIN MOTHER

Neither Horus the Elder nor Horus the Younger were born to a virgin mother. Instead, both had "god" parents:

- Horus the Elder was born to Nut (the sky god) and Geb[60] (the earth god).
- Horus the Younger was conceived through the union of Osiris and his sister, Isis[61].

---

[59] Bill Maher, 07/21/2017, "Bill Maher: Religulous (2008)—Transcript," *Scrapsfromtheloft.com*.
[60] Joshua J. Mark, "Horus," *World History Encyclopedia*, March 16, 2016.
[61] Mark, "Horus."

The claim that Horus the Younger had a virgin mother originated with D.M. Murdock, who tried to argue for a nonexistent similarity between paganism and Christianity by saying that Horus's mother, Isis, had *"born-again virginity."* She called Isis a *'perpetual virgin'*[62] regardless of her previous relationships.[63] The one quote that Murdock used to justify her claim was a quotation from the philosopher Porphyry of Tyre,[64] where he said: *"In all these ways, then, the power of the earth finds an interpretation and is worshipped: as a virgin and Hestia, she holds the centre; as a mother, she nourishes ..."*[65]

Timing is a problem for using this quotation to support that (1) Isis was a virgin when giving birth to Horus, and (2) Christianity stole it from paganism. This quotation is from Eusebius, who is citing Porphyry. Why is that a problem? Primarily because Porphyry cannot be the source for the Christian doctrine of the virgin birth—he lived from 234-305 AD! So, unless the early Christians had a DeLorean with a 1.21 gigawatt flux capacitor to shoot into the future, rip off Porphyry, and then shoot back to their time, it would have been impossible. Something stated three centuries in the future cannot be the source that one copies from—you cannot copy a story that doesn't exist yet.

BAPTIZED BY ANUP THE BAPTIZER WHO WAS LATER BEHEADED

How do I say this nicely? This is complete and total BUNK! This supposed "theory" came from the mind of English poet Gerald Massey in his publication, "Egyptian Book of the Dead."[66] Feel

[62] D. M. Murdock, *Christ in Egypt: The Horus-Jesus Connection*, 2009: 178, 191.
[63] Blake Giunta, nd, "Was Horus Born of a Virgin (Isis-Mary)?" *Belief Map*.
[64] Eyjólfur Emilsson, "Porphyry," *The Stanford Encyclopedia of Philosophy* (Spring 2022 Edition), Edward N. Zalta (ed.)
[65] Porphyry, and Edwin Hamilton Gifford, trans. *On Images*, Fragment 7.
[66] Gerald Massey, *Egyptian Book of the Dead and the Ancient Mysteries of Amenta*, 1994.

free to do your own search; you will find no evidence of Horus having been baptized or of Anup the Baptizer.

TEMPTED IN THE DESERT

You'll find this claim in a companion guide to the film *Zeitgeist*. It's easy to say that "with over 1,000 theatrical screenings in 60 countries and 30 languages, viewed by millions on the internet,"[67] this distortion of the truth has significantly influenced many in the culture. In the *Zeitgeist* study guide, you'll read that: *"As does Satan with Jesus, Set (aka Seth) attempts to kill Horus. Set is the 'god of the desert' who battles Horus, while Jesus is tempted in the desert by Satan" (p. 23).*[68]

But, as Jon Sorensen wrote: *"Doing battle with the 'god of the desert' is not the same as being tempted while alone in the desert; and according to the Gospel accounts, Satan did not attempt to kill Jesus there"* (Matthew 4; Mark 1:12–13; Luke 4:1–13).[69]

HEALED THE SICK, CAST OUT DEMONS, WALKED ON WATER

These supposed similarities come from the Cippus of Horus, a stone carving dating to the 4th century B.C. Here we read about a magical cure used on the infant Horus because he got sick while hiding in the marshes with his mother, Isis.[70] Please don't trust me; read this for yourself. What is carved on this stone is NOTHING like what is written in the Word of God. Horus did not travel around the country healing the blind and sick, and there's NOTHING about casting out demons or walking on water. We will return

[67] *Zeitgeist: The Series, directed by Peter Joseph* (SidewaysFilms, 2007), 6:48:00.
[68] Jon Sorensen, nd, "Horus Manure: Debunking the Jesus/Horus Connection," *Strange Notions*.
[69] Sorensen, "Horus Manure."
[70] Unknown, *Magical Stela* (Cippus of Horus): Late Period, stone sculpture.

to this stone monument in a second to answer another claim. Hang tight!

RAISED ASAR FROM THE DEAD

If I may be so bold, I'd highly encourage you to read this history for yourself again. You can find a copy of the resurrection story from the Albany Institute of History & Art at wondriumdaily.com/isis-and-osiris-death-and-rebirth-in-ancient-egypt/. Here's the "Cliff Notes" response:

> Horus did not resurrect anyone. His mother, Isis, resurrected her husband/brother, Osiris, from the dead because her other brother, Seth, was jealous and killed him. She magically brought him back from the dead after finding his body, which had been cut up into 14 pieces and spread around the countryside. Isis and her sister searched the countryside to find 13 parts. Unfortunately, the crucial piece necessary for procreation was no longer available as a fish had eaten it. Nevertheless, Isis transformed into a falcon and flew around Osiris to get pregnant with Horus. (Sorry, I know this is very similar to Christian teaching, which makes it very hard to differentiate between the two stories!) After this was accomplished, he had to go to the underworld because he was incomplete, and this was where he would reign.[71]

Don't just take my word for it; read the history yourself.

CRUCIFIED

Short answer, NO! There is no evidence that Horus died by crucifixion. Zero, zilch, nada! According to one source, Spencer McDaniel:

---

[71] Mark, "Horus."

> *Bill Maher claims that a myth of Horus being crucified was written down around 1280 BC, but the ancient Egyptians during the New Kingdom actually did not practice crucifixion, and they probably did not even know what crucifixion was. In fact, we have no reliable records of crucifixion having been practiced anywhere in the world at all at that time.*[72]

RESURRECTED THREE DAYS LATER

I told you we'd return to the Cippus of Horus stone monument, so here we are. In a nutshell, the account of Horus dying and resurrecting goes as follows:

- First, after killing Osiris, Set(h) captures Isis and puts her in a cave, possibly to convince her to marry him so that he can seize the kingdom.
- Isis gives birth to Horus in the cave.
- Then the god Thoth comes to Isis in the cave to help her:

  > "*Thoth now appeared to her and advised her to hide with her unborn child, and to bring him forth in secret, and he promised her that her son should succeed in due course to his father's throne. With the help of Thoth, she escaped from her captivity, and went forth accompanied by the Seven Scorpion-goddesses.*"[73]

- After escaping the cave, Horus is stung by a scorpion and dies.
- Then, "*The grief of the woman was so bitter and sympa-*

[72] Spencer McDaniel, "Was Jesus Copied Off the Egyptian God Horus?" *Tales of Times Forgotten*, November 24, 2019.
[73] Nd. "VIII. The Legend of the Death and Resurrection of Horus, and Other Magical Texts," *Sacred-texts.com*: IXXIV.

> *thy-compelling that Isis laid her hands on the child, and, having uttered one of her most potent spells over him, the poison of the scorpion ran out of his body, and the child came to life again.*"[74]

So, there you go. You can't tell the difference between the resurrection of Horus and Jesus! (Sorry, sarcasm is my love language!)

The truth is there's NOTHING similar between these two accounts. But wait, there's more! Since I have a little more space left (but not enough to do an *in-depth* explanation of claims that Attis, Krishna, or Mithras' stories were the basis for the narrative about Jesus' life), I will address one last claim that's typically made for all the aforementioned gods: They were all born on December 25th! Oh, my!

BORN ON DECEMBER 25TH

Depends! Horus the Elder was not born on December 25th. He was born during the "Epagomenal Days" in July. Horus the Younger *was* supposedly born on December 25th. But who cares—we all KNOW that Jesus was NOT born on December 25th[75]. So that means that Horus the Elder has the most in common with Jesus—neither of them was born on December 25th. And, for the sake of clarification, neither was Krishna or Mithras. Wow! What are we going to do, Christian? We can't trust Christ is who He claims to be because He shares a non-December 25th birthday with Horus the Elder, Krishna,[76] and Mithras![77]

---

[74] "The Legend of Horus," pp. IXXIV–IXXV.
[75] See Chapter 8 of this book, "Was Jesus Actually Born on December 25th?" by Frank Figueroa, Jr.
[76] Today Krishna is remembered in the Hindu Calendar first and foremost on his birthday, which is celebrated in August or September in a festival called Janmashtami. (Kristin Johnston Largen, *Baby Krishna, Infant Christ: A Comparative Theology of Salvation* [Maryknoll, NY: Orbis Books, 2011], 44).
[77] Tertullian, "Mithras and Christianity," *Tertullian.org*.

By the way, please allow me to give you another similarity between Jesus and Mithras. Yes, they have another feature in common. Both *were* born of a virgin! So how do we handle that? It's pretty simple; quite honestly, Jesus was born of the Virgin Mary, and Mithra's mom didn't have a name because he was supposedly born from a rock (and rocks are virgins, technically speaking)![78]

All the evidence we have to address these claims shows that it's actually the other way around. The pagan gods were losing followers to Christianity, so they borrowed from Christian teachings. One of the strongest arguments for that is the resurrection of Christ. According to Swedish scholar and non-Christian Professor T.N.D Mettinger of Lund University, "the consensus among modern scholars—*nearly universal*—is that there were no dying and rising gods that preceded Christianity. They all post-dated the first century."[79] Professor Mettinger also stated, "There is, as far as I am aware, no *prima facie* evidence that the death and resurrection of Jesus is a mythological construct, drawing on the myths and rites of the dying and rising gods of the surrounding world."[80]

So, there you have it. Jesus did not rip off any of these pitiful gods. God is who He claimed to be. He loves us the way that He claimed He did. He is the only God, and He loved us so much that while we were yet sinners, He came and died for us so that we might have the opportunity for forgiveness and to spend eternity with Him in a real place called heaven. Choose this day whom you will follow. But, as for me and my household, we will serve the Lord to the best of our ability and share His love with as many as possible.

Stay Bold!

---

[78] CIMRM 344, 1914,"Mithras rock-born, H.0.63," marble statue, Mithraeum, *Terullian.org*, San Clemente, Rome.
[79] Lee Strobel, "Was the resurrection of Jesus a story taken from mythology?" *Bible Gateway Blog*, April 4, 2013.
[80] Strobel, "Was resurrection taken from mythology?"

CHAPTER 7

DO THE NARRATIVES OF JESUS' BIRTH CONTRADICT ONE ANOTHER?

David Madsen

At Christmastime, we often see Nativity sets that include baby Jesus, Mary, and Joseph in a stable with shepherds on one side and wise men on the other. But Scripture doesn't indicate that the shepherds and wise men came to see the Christ child at the same time—in fact, Matthew's Gospel says nothing about the shepherds, and Luke's Gospel says nothing about the wise men. Such differences in the two accounts of Christ's birth—as well as some differences between the Gospel accounts and other historical documents—have led skeptics to object that there are contradictions in the biblical records. However, a closer look at these arguments indicates that *differences* in the accounts of Matthew and Luke are not *discrepancies*.

OBJECTION #1: MATTHEW'S AND LUKE'S VARIED ACCOUNTS OF CHRIST'S BIRTH CONTRADICT EACH OTHER.

Although the accounts of Matthew and Luke do include different details of Christ's nativity, the truth is that the major events are the same in both:

- Angelic announcements preceded Jesus' birth (Matthew 1:20–21; Luke 1:26–31).
- Jesus was born in Bethlehem (Matthew 2:1; Luke 2:4–7).
- Jesus was virgin-born (Matthew 1:22–23; Luke 1:34–35).
- Jesus' conception was of the Holy Ghost (Matthew 1:18, 20; Luke 1:35).
- Mary and Joseph were an engaged couple at the time of the angelic announcement and not married until after the virgin conception of Christ (Matthew 1:24–25; Luke 1:26–27).
- Jesus is described as the "Savior" (Matthew 1:21; Luke 2:11).
- Jesus was proclaimed to be the promised Messiah of Old Testament prophecy (Matthew 2:4-6; Luke 2:25–32).
- The events of Jesus' birth happened during Herod's reign (Matthew 2:1; Luke 1:5).
- Mary, Joseph, and Jesus settled in Nazareth after the events of the Nativity (Matthew 2:23; Luke 2:39).

And although Matthew's and Luke's Gospels differ in some details, an omission of an event in one or the other accounts does not mean a contradiction. Matthew's and Luke's accounts must be given the same latitude as other biographies: no two biographies on a subject ever include the exact information. For example, a recent biography of Abraham Lincoln by David Herbert Donald contains 714 pages, while another biography of Lincoln by Josiah Gilbert Holland has only 471 pages. No honest critic would say that omissions in the shorter biography indicate a contradiction between the two.

In addition, both Matthew and Luke were credible sources to relate the events of Christ's birth. Matthew was an apostle who spent three years with Jesus (Matthew 10:3, Acts 1:13) and knew Mary, Jesus' mother (Acts 1:14), so Matthew likely had first-hand accounts of the miraculous birth. Apologist Josh McDowell also points out that Matthew was a "former tax collector, a man accustomed to keeping accurate records."[81]

Although not an apostle, Luke was an equally credible source about the Nativity. Luke was a companion to Paul, who knew Christ's apostles personally and likely related the events of Christ's birth he received from first-hand witnesses. Luke's accuracy as a historian in both his Gospel and Acts has been well-documented, with historian William Ramsay noting that "Luke's history is unsurpassed in its trustworthiness."[82]

Also, Luke relates that he was familiar with other accounts of Christ's life—one of which was probably Matthew's Gospel. Luke's Gospel notes, "Many have undertaken to compile a narrative of the things that have been accomplished among us, just as those who from the beginning were eyewitnesses and ministers of the word have delivered them to us" (Luke 1:1–2). Scholars unanimously agree that Luke's Gospel was written after Matthew's and Mark's, and it's reasonable to conclude that the narratives that Luke refers to are the Gospel accounts from those two men. If Luke was indeed familiar with Matthew's Gospel (as Ramsay also argues[83]), he most likely added details omitted by Matthew to give a more complete picture of the events surrounding the Nativity.

---

[81] Josh McDowell, *The New Evidence That Demands a Verdict*, 296.
[82] Josh McDowell, *The New Evidence That Demands a Verdict*, 63.
[83] William Ramsay, *Was Christ Born in Bethlehem?*, 79.

OBJECTION #2: MATTHEW'S ACCOUNT SAYS MARY AND JOSEPH WENT TO EGYPT AFTER CHRIST'S BIRTH, BUT LUKE'S ACCOUNT CONTRADICTS THIS AND SAYS THEY WENT TO NAZARETH.

It's true that Matthew's account includes the flight to Egypt, and Luke's doesn't. But, once again, Luke's omission of this event doesn't mean a contradiction with Matthew. Both Luke's and Matthew's accounts clearly show that Jesus was born in Bethlehem and grew up in Nazareth. Luke's omission of the flight to Egypt is similar to what Scripture summarizes elsewhere. For example, the creation of mankind in Genesis 1 gives such a summary: "Male and female created He them" (Genesis 1:27). If this is all we were given about the origin of humans, we would be left to assume the first man and woman were made at the same time. However, Genesis 2 shows an expanded version of the story, explaining that Adam was first created from dust and Eve was formed later from his rib. Moses doesn't contradict himself in writing Genesis 1 and 2; he simply adds more detail in Chapter 2 based on the context of the passage. Likewise, Matthew's inclusion of the flight to Egypt is consistent with his narrative's focus on King Herod (including Herod's visit by the wise men and Herod's massacre of Bethlehem's children)—likely contrasting the despotic earthly king with the promised heavenly King. Luke's Gospel, however, does not focus on Herod, so the detour to Egypt would not be relevant to his account. Again, since Luke most likely had access to Matthew's Gospel, it makes no sense that he would intentionally write a contradictory account. Theologian James Orr notes that "the two narratives, while independent, are not contradictory, but are really complementary. Matthew supplements Luke's silence about Joseph and the removal of his difficulties; Luke supplies what is lacking in Matthew about the thoughts and feelings of Mary. We must treat the series of incidents in both Gospels, therefore, together; they stand or fall as one set of facts."[84]

OBJECTION #3: THE GENEALOGIES SURROUNDING THE BIRTH OF CHRIST IN MATTHEW AND LUKE CONTRADICT EACH OTHER.

Though the genealogies of Christ in Matthew 1 and Luke 4 contain some differences, they both make the same main point: Jesus Christ was a descendant of Abraham *and* David. Not only was Christ the fulfillment of God's promise that the world would be blessed through Abraham's line (Genesis 22:18), but He also fulfilled the promise that the Messiah would come from David's royal line (Isaiah 9:7).

Skeptics' biggest issue with the genealogical records is that Matthew's Gospel lists Joseph's father as "Jacob," whereas Luke's Gospel lists Joseph's father as "Heli." But the differences in the genealogies likely reflect the separate lines of Joseph (recorded in Matthew's Gospel) and Mary (recorded in Luke's Gospel), with Luke's "Joseph, which was the son of Heli" best understood as "Joseph, which was the son-*in-law* of Heli" (Genealogies in Jewish culture typically traced ancestry through the males of the family line, and this is probably the reason Mary is not mentioned.). Such an idea is supported by the Talmud, the collection of Jewish rabbinical commentaries on the Torah compiled in the centuries after Christ, in which Mary is recorded as being the daughter of Heli,[85] making Heli Joseph's father-in-law. Bible scholar C.I. Scofield noted, "[Joseph] could not be by natural generation the son both of Jacob and of Heli. But in Luke, it is not said that Heli *begat* Joseph, so that the natural explanation is that Joseph was the son-in-law of Heli, who was (like himself), a descendant of David.

[84] James Orr, *The Virgin Birth of Christ*, 77.
[85] Tony Pearce, "Messiah to be descended from David," *The Messiah Factor*.

That he should in that case be called "son of Heli" ... would be in accord with Jewish usage."[86]

... THESE INSPIRED ACCOUNTS DO NOT CONTRADICT ONE ANOTHER BUT ARE IN HARMONY—DIFFERENCES DO NOT MEAN DISCREPANCIES.

Luke's genealogy following Mary's line is certainly consistent with his highlighting of Mary's experience in the Christmas narrative, as he records the angelic announcement to Mary (Luke 1:26–38), Mary's encounter with Elizabeth after the virgin conception (Luke 1:39–56), and Mary's later being addressed by Simeon at Christ's presentation in the temple (Luke 2:34); it is no coincidence that Luke notes that "Mary kept all these things, and pondered them in her heart" (Luke 2:19). Matthew's Gospel, on the other hand, seems to follow Joseph's experience, as he highlights Joseph's struggle with understanding Mary's conception (Matthew 1:18–19) and Joseph being visited by angels on three occasions (Matthew 1:20–21; 2:13, 19). Therefore, the two different genealogies are consistent with the context of the Gospels in which they are recorded.

[86] John R. Rice, *The King of the Jews: A Commentary on the Gospel According to Matthew*, 24–25.

OBJECTION #4: MATTHEW'S AND LUKE'S ACCOUNTS CONTRADICT OTHER HISTORICAL RECORDS.

Skeptics accuse Luke of inaccuracy in 1:5 and 2:2 by recording that Herod (king of Galilee) and Quirinius (governor of Syria) ruled simultaneously since Jewish historian Josephus records that Quirinius' reign began in AD 6, long after Herod died in 4 BC—which would mean the two did not rule at the same time.[87] However, there are several good reasons to believe that Luke was historically correct:

First, it's possible that more than one Quirinius ruled Syria. The late Professor Jerry Vardaman of the Cobb Institute of Archaeology of Mississippi State University discovered a coin with the name "Quirinius" inscribed on it, placing him as the proconsul of Syria during the time of Herod, meaning there were two men with the same name who ruled Syria at different times: the Quirinius that Josephus records and the one Luke records.[88]

Second, it's possible that Quirinius governed Syria more than once. Ramsay noted the discovery of a marble fragment in Rome in 1764 bearing the inscription of a Roman official that matched the historical description of Quirinius, though the fragment does not include a name. If the inscription does indeed refer to Quirinius, it notably states that he governed Syria *twice*. Ramsay concludes that Quirinius' first reign was the one Luke referenced, and his second reign was the one Josephus referenced.[89]

Third, it's possible that a Greek-to-English translation error in Luke's record could resolve the supposed discrepancy. Greek

---

[87] Jack Finnegan, *Light from the Ancient Past*, 258–259.
[88] Lee Strobel, *The Case for Christmas*, 48.
[89] William Ramsay, *Was Christ Born in Bethlehem?*, 245–246.

scholar Nigel Turner from the University of Edinburgh argues that the Greek word *protos*, typically translated as "first" in English, could also be translated as "before." This would indicate that the census of Herod's time was *before* Quirinius was governor of Syria"[90] and would be consistent with Josephus' record.

Skeptics also accuse Matthew's account of being inaccurate since there's no extra-biblical record of Herod's massacre of infants from Matthew 2:16–18. But, once again, omissions do not mean contradictions. Although no extra-biblical record of this event has been found, Matthew's account is consistent with Herod's despotic reign. Bruce Scott, author of *The Feasts of Israel: Seasons of the Messiah,* notes Herod's penchant for murder: "Herod had no qualms about killing. He killed the 2,000 survivors of five cities that had rebelled against him. He had his brother-in-law drowned. He executed his uncle, his wife's grandfather, his wife, his mother-in-law, and three sons. He murdered faithful followers, servants, friends, soldiers, pious men, and relatives."[91] It's also possible that the event Matthew records was on a smaller scale than commonly thought. Dr. John McRay, the author of *Archeology and the New Testament*, notes that Bethlehem was a small rural town that most likely had a small number of infants under two years old, so the killing of a handful of children may not have seemed a significant enough tragedy for extra-biblical historians to record given Herod's more infamous atrocities.[92]

Skeptics further claim the census of Luke 2:1 is not historically accurate since Josephus records the census under Quirinius as taking place in AD 6—many years after Herod's death. However, Dr. Darrell Bock, contributing author to *The Holman Apologetics Commentary on the Bible: The Gospels and Acts*, argues that Luke's census may have been part of a longer census: "This census

---

[90] Jeffrey Sheler, *Is the Bible True?*, 197.
[91] Bruce Scott, "Herod the Not-So-Great," *Israel My Glory* (November/December 2006).
[92] Lee Strobel, *The Case for Christmas*, 51–52.

took place somewhere between 6 and 4 BC—at least the beginning mechanizations of it—but it wasn't actually executed until we got to Quirinius. In other words, he's the one who got the data, put it together, presented it for Rome, and Rome actually began to make use of it for taxation under Quirinius. So this is a long process."[93]

Yet another possibility has been proposed by Professor John H. Rhodes of Concordia University, Chicago, who argues that Josephus' dating of the census—not Luke's—is wrong. He argues that Josephus' record of a census is a "mistaken duplication" of the historical event that happened much earlier in time, vindicating Luke's record.[94] Again, Luke's accuracy as a historian must be considered in this regard. As well-known historian A.N. Sherwin-White noted, "For the New Testament of Acts, the confirmation of historicity is overwhelming ... any attempt to reject its basic historicity, even in matters of detail, must now appear absurd. Roman historians have long taken it for granted."[95] The important point is that such censuses, as recorded by Luke, do have precedent in the ancient world. According to historical records, Caesar Augustus initiated three censuses around the time of Christ's birth,[96] and with the limited amount of extra-biblical documentation still existing in the censuses of the ancient world, there's no reason to question the accuracy of Luke's record on this point.

CONCLUSION

Although there are differences in Luke's and Matthew's records of the Christmas story, we can have confidence that these inspired accounts do not contradict one another but are in harmony—differences do not mean discrepancies. Likewise, where

[93] Mikel Del Rosario, "Did Luke Get the Christmas Story Wrong?" Voice, Dallas Theological Seminary (December 24, 2013).
[94] John H. Rhodes, "Josephus Misdated the Census of Quirinius," *Journal of the Evangelical Theological Society* 54, no. 1 (March 2011), 65–87.
[95] A. N. Sherwin-White, *Roman Society and Roman Law in the New Testament*, 189.
[96] Darrell Bock, *Luke, BECNT*, ed. Moises Silva., vol. 1, 904.

the Gospel accounts and extra-biblical historical sources disagree, there are ample reasons to believe that the biblical account is trustworthy. Ultimately, God has given us an authoritative and accurate picture of the historical event of Christ's birth.

CHAPTER 8

WAS JESUS ACTUALLY BORN ON DECEMBER 25TH?

Frank Figueroa, Jr.

It is a common assumption that the birth of Jesus Christ happened on December 25th. In fact, many countries have a national holiday to commemorate it: Christmas. The English word *Christmas* ("mass on Christ's Day") is a term more recent in its origins, which we will cover shortly. But was Jesus actually born on December 25th? To put it succinctly, probably not, and although not impossible, it seems highly unlikely.

The first recorded year of Christmas celebrated on December 25th was 336 AD, during the time of the Roman Emperor Constantine. At this time, the Bishop of Jerusalem wrote to the bishop of Rome, asking him to determine the actual day of Jesus' birth. But actually, no one knew for sure the day or even the exact year of Jesus' birth. There is much speculation on how this date was chosen but suffice it to say, it is the most commonly accepted date in the world to recognize the birth of Jesus of Nazareth.

Before we begin, I want to offer one caveat . . . Nothing in this chapter can be established dogmatically. Because we don't have biblical or historical documentation of the actual day Jesus was born, everything we will discuss here will be based on opinion. Yes, there may be some biblical texts to substantiate those opinions, but there is no clear-cut, beyond-a-shadow-of-a-doubt way that the actual day of Jesus' birth can be determined, which must be stated as we dive into this topic.

That being said, one problem with December 25th being the actual date that Christ was born is that it would be unusual, given other narratives in the Christmas account. For instance, Luke 2:8 tells us, "Now there were in the same country shepherds living out in the fields, keeping watch over their flock by night." In that part of the world (Israel), it is pretty cold (low 40s, just above freezing) during December, and the fields are usually far less productive. So it is doubtful that the shepherds lived with their flocks in the fields during this time of the year. The more normative practice was to keep the flocks in the fields from spring to autumn and bring them in during the winter.

Also, winter would likely be an especially difficult time for Joseph and Mary (who was quite pregnant) to travel the long distance from Nazareth to Bethlehem (80–90 miles). We are not sure how they traveled, but winter weather would have made it exponentially more problematic. Cold weather and poor road conditions due to rain during this season would have added to the difficulties. I am not saying that they could not have accomplished this due to environmental conditions, but it would have significantly intensified an already exhausting journey.

The most plausible alternative time that some scholars have put forth for the birth of Jesus would be around late September. To see how they arrive at that conclusion, let's look at Luke 2:1–7:

> *And it came to pass in those days that a decree went out from Caesar Augustus that all the world should be registered. This census first took place while Quirinius was governing Syria. So all went to be registered, everyone to his own city.*
>
> *Joseph also went up from Galilee, out of the city of Nazareth, into Judea, to the city of David, which is called Bethlehem, because he was of the house and lineage of David, to be registered with Mary, his betrothed wife, who was with child. So it was, that while they were there, the days were completed for her to be delivered. And she brought forth her firstborn Son, and wrapped Him in swaddling cloths, and laid Him in a manger, because there was no room for them in the inn.*

Cities took a census when most of their citizens would be at or returning to their hometown, which was no exception in this case. Because of this, most census statistics were recorded during major Jewish feasts when such travel was common. The belief among many is that because the Jewish Feast of Tabernacles was held in late September, this would have been a time when Joseph and Mary would have returned to Bethlehem.

Another line of reasoning that is used to validate the late September birth is based on the information we find in the Bible regarding the birth of John the Baptist. Luke tells us that John the Baptist's father, Zacharias, was a priest in the priestly division of Abijah. Luke 1:5 "There was in the days of Herod, the king of Judea, a certain priest named Zacharias, of the division of Abijah. His wife *was* of the daughters of Aaron, and her name *was* Elizabeth." It was his turn to serve in the temple when something amazing happened:

Luke 1:8–13

> *So it was, that while he was serving as priest before God in the order of his division, according to the custom of the priesthood, his lot fell to burn incense when he went into the temple of the Lord. And the whole multitude of the people was praying outside at the hour of incense. Then an angel of the Lord appeared to him, standing on the right side of the altar of incense. And when Zacharias saw him, he was troubled, and fear fell upon him. But the angel said to him, 'Do not be afraid, Zacharias, for your prayer is heard; and your wife Elizabeth will bear you a son, and you shall call his name John.'*

Notice that he was serving in the temple when he was approached by the angel Gabriel and told that his wife, Elizabeth, was going to conceive and bear a son. After Zacharias completed his time of temple service, he returned home, and his wife became pregnant, just as the angel had said. Six months later, the same angel went to Mary, Elizabeth's cousin, to tell her that she would have a child also, but her child was going to be the Messiah, and God would be His Father:

Luke 1:26–37

Now in the sixth month the angel Gabriel was sent by God to a city of Galilee named Nazareth, to a virgin betrothed to a man whose name was Joseph, of the house of David. The virgin's name was Mary. And having come in, the angel said to her, 'Rejoice, highly favored one, the Lord is with you; blessed are you among women!' But when she saw him, she was troubled at his saying, and considered what manner of greeting this was. Then the angel said to her, 'Do not be afraid, Mary, for you have found favor with God. And behold, you will conceive in your womb and bring forth a Son, and shall call His name JESUS. He will be great, and will be called the Son of the Highest; and the Lord God will give Him the throne of His father David. And He will reign over the house of Jacob forever, and of His kingdom there will be no end.' Then Mary said to the angel, 'How can this be, since I do not know a man?' And the angel answered and said to her, 'The Holy Spirit will come upon you, and the power of the Highest will overshadow you; therefore, also, that Holy One who is to be born will be called the Son of God. Now indeed, Elizabeth your relative has also conceived a son in her old age; and this is now the sixth month for her who was called barren. For with God nothing will be impossible.'

If we use all the information regarding Zacharias, history has recorded that the priests in the division of Abijah served in the temple from June 13 through June 19.[97] If Elizabeth conceived shortly after Zacharias returned home, she would have been six months pregnant around the end of December. We know that the

[97] "Was Jesus actually born in September?" *Got Questions.*

angel Gabriel appeared to Mary during the sixth month of Elizabeth's pregnancy. So if we assume that Mary became pregnant shortly after the angel Gabriel's announcement to her, then Jesus would have been born approximately nine months later, potentially in late September: right at the time of the Feast of Tabernacles.

I want to reiterate that these are all speculations. We cannot be exact as to the dates of Zacharias' service in the temple, although we have a pretty good estimate of the dates given. We also have to remember that while David created the priestly divisions, they were not enacted until his son, Solomon, was reigning (1 Chronicles 24:7-18). In addition, there was a reset of the rotations while the Jews were in Babylonian exile, according to Ezra chapter 2. So this speculation is not without its own set of problems.

However, it is plausible that John the Baptist was conceived in late June after the angel Gabriel visited Zacharias and Elizabeth. Six months later, in late December, Mary would have become pregnant and given birth in late September, allowing many pieces of the puzzle to fit together quite nicely.

Does this tarnish the December 25 date, then? Instead of questioning whether Jesus was born on December 25th or not, let's use this date to commemorate His birth, regardless of when it happened. December 25th then becomes a day where we all agree to stop what we are doing and remember that Christ humbled Himself and was born in a manger to carry out the work of redemption. What better way to celebrate the day than by remembering the fulfillment of God's promises? First, to a young woman who would bring the Messiah into the world. Second, to all of us as sinful human beings, people who needed a Savior to be reconciled to God and forgiven of our sins. All of this happened by God's power and in His timing, whatever the date may be. Let's not get hung up on the things we don't know for sure and allow that to cause us to miss the glorious truth of what we do know for sure:

Luke 2:10–11

Then the angel said to them, "Do not be afraid, for behold,

I bring you good tidings of great joy which will be to all people.

For there is born to you this day in the city of David

a Savior, who is Christ the Lord."

PART THREE

MEANING-MAKERS OF THE CHRISTMAS STORY

CHAPTER 9

WHAT DOES IT MATTER THAT MARY WAS A VIRGIN?

Dave Glander

What color should the sanctuary walls be? Should we allow guitars and drums during worship, or only a piano? Is baptism only valid by full submersion, or is sprinkling acceptable? Is communion to be done with self-serve cups or a loaf of bread? Wine or grape juice? Believe it or not, these questions have caused literal splits between denominations and churches throughout time . . . but are they that important? Are they essential to the Christian faith as a salvation issue? What are the essentials to the Christian faith that every believer must profess to have accurate and genuine knowledge, understanding, and belief to truly be saved?

es·sen·tial
adjective

absolutely necessary; extremely important.

THE DEITY OF CHRIST JESUS IS ARGUABLY THE MOST ESSENTIAL DOCTRINE OF THE CHRISTIAN FAITH.

While there are several essentials to the Christian faith, like salvation by grace through faith in Jesus alone, the inerrancy of Scripture, the gospel, monotheism, and the Trinity, the deity of Christ Jesus is arguably the most essential doctrine of the Christian faith. In fact, the doctrine of the deity of Christ must be fully understood to grasp the gospel message of salvation. Organically built into the qualifications for His deity are essential details of His life, many of which are of utmost importance. Which section of the Jordan River He was baptized in, or what exact year He was born, are not those essentials! Essential details that must be acknowledged include the virgin birth, His sinless life, His sacrificial death, and His resurrection! Taking away any of those four components will severely affect the true Gospel. [I would add there is a fifth element, His imminent return, but that's another topic altogether.] So, regarding the original question for this chapter, the virgin birth isn't just one of the essentials; it is the very first one of extreme importance and is absolutely necessary. Let's see why!

THE ELEPHANT IN THE ROOM

To give this question an honest examination, we must address the most common objection to the idea of the virgin birth as told by the prophet Isaiah. In Isaiah 7:14, we read the following prophecy: *"Therefore the Lord himself will give you a sign. Behold, the virgin shall conceive and bear a son, and shall call his name Immanuel."*

The Hebrew word used here is *"almah,"* meaning *a young woman or a virgin*. Of course, skeptics will try to say that *"young woman"* is the main idea meant to be translated and not necessarily a virgin. However, when you take the seven times this word is used in the Hebrew Old Testament [OT], you see the following uses: *girl (1), maid (1), maiden (1), maidens (3), virgin (1).* "Maid," "maiden," "maidens," and "virgin" constitute six of the seven references. According to Merriam-Webster.com, the meaning of the word *maiden* is "an unmarried girl or woman: virgin: never yet mated."

Think about the term for a new ship that has never sailed the waters: its very first voyage is called its "Maiden Journey." At the time Isaiah's passage was written, everyone would have understood that even if translated as "maiden," Isaiah was referring to a virgin because, at that time, an unmarried woman would most certainly have never been with a man!

To put a nail in the coffin for this supposed objection, we'll look at the word translated into Greek at the time of the writing of the Greek Septuagint. The Septuagint is a translation of the Hebrew OT into Greek by seventy Jewish scholars. This was due to the influence of the Greek language becoming more common around the second and third centuries BC.[98] When the Jewish scholars came to Isaiah's word, "almah," they used the Greek word *"Parthenos,"* which translates to *a maiden, virgin.* As you can see, in Greek, there is no confusion about what the word means, which is why when Mark penned the fulfillment of Isaiah's prophecy concerning the historic birth of Jesus in Mark 1:23, he used the same Greek word: *"Behold, the virgin [Parthenos] shall conceive and bear a son, and they shall call his name 'Immanuel' (which means God with us)."*

By the time Christ was born, the idea of His "strange birth" would've already been accepted and understood by the people liv-

[98] For more information on the importance of the Septuagint, go to gotquestions.org/septuagint.html.

ing at that time. The Bible talks about those around Him who knew that something wasn't quite normal about Jesus' arrival on earth. One time, when Jesus began teaching in the synagogue, some said of Him, *"Is not this the carpenter, the son of Mary..."* (Mark 6:3a). Referring to Him as the *"son of Mary"* was a direct accusation that He was not Joseph's child, considering that at that time, names were always credited to the father.

Another time the Scribes and the Pharisees said to Him, *"We were not born of sexual immorality..."* [Other translations: *"We are not illegitimate children."*] *". . . We have one Father—even God"* (John 8:41b.) Once again, their claim that He was an illegitimate child born out of sexual immorality was another stab at Jesus' birth, not understanding that He was actually conceived by the Holy Spirit! And I love how Jesus responded to them. He said, *"If God were your Father, you would love me, for I came from God, and I am here."* (John 8:42a). He literally told them that He fulfilled Isaiah's prophecy by coming here directly from God without the help of an earthly father—Boom . . . mic drop! Consider also that the virgin birth story comes from Mary herself. As Sean McDowell so clearly argues, as follows:

> *Also, when Mary turned up pregnant, why would she have insisted she was a virgin? She knew that such a story would certainly be considered too wild to believe; why didn't she come up with something more credible? She could have concocted an excuse to make herself look innocent, or at least to put part of the blame on someone else. She could have claimed she was raped, or that Joseph had pressured her into yielding to his desire. He would have known better, but no one else would have. But instead of a rational explanation that would fit the known laws of nature, she told people she was pregnant by God's Holy Spirit. Why would she have said such a thing when*

it was the least believable of explanations? Only one reason makes sense. It was true.[99]

The claim made by modern skeptics that the Bible doesn't say Jesus would be born of a virgin has been debunked . . . Adios!

ON TO THE REAL MATTER AT HAND!

The Bible clearly states, *"Sin came into the world through one man, and death through sin, and so death spread to all men because all sinned."* (Romans 5:12). Did you catch that? Through one MAN, sin came into the world. To fully understand this, we must go back to the beginning. Genesis 1:15–17 tells us of the first human to ever be created by God during the six days of creation. *"The LORD God took* ***the man*** *and put* ***him*** *in the garden of Eden to work it and keep it. And the LORD God commanded* ***the man****, saying, '****You*** *may surely eat of every tree of the garden, but of the tree of the knowledge of good and evil* ***you*** *shall not eat, for in the day that* ***you*** *eat of it* ***you*** *shall surely die.'"* [Emphasis added] At this point in creation, Adam was alone. He alone was the one whom God gave this commandment to! In verse 18 we see that "the LORD God said, 'It is not good that the man should be alone; I will make him a helper fit for him.'" Eve was NOT even alive yet when God made the agreement with Adam, which is why Romans tells us that it is through the man that sin has entered the world because it was through the first man that God had the agreement with. It was Adam's job to protect his new wife from the serpent influencing her to eat the forbidden fruit. To further back this up, 1 Timothy 2:14 tells us, *"Adam was not deceived, but the woman was deceived."* Adam KNEW what he was doing when he violated his agreement, unlike Eve, who was deceived into doing so!

[99] Sean McDowell, "Is there Evidence Jesus Was Born of a Virgin?" *SeanMcDowell.org*, December 23, 2017.

JESUS HAD TO BE BORN OF A VIRGIN SO THAT THE SIN CURSE UPON ALL HUMANITY WAS NOT PASSED ONTO HIM THROUGH AN EARTHLY FATHER.

This means that Jesus HAD to be born of a virgin so that the sin curse upon all humanity was not passed onto Him through an earthly father. Amazingly, God already had a plan for this and let us know in Genesis 3:15. When God told Satan his punishment for deceiving Eve in the garden. He said, *"I will put enmity between you and the woman, and between your offspring and her offspring; he shall bruise your head, and you shall bruise his heel."* The Hebrew word for offspring is *"zera,"* often translated as *"seed."* Here's the thing: without the aid of a man, women can't have a *"seed"* or *"offspring"* by themselves. "Human reproduction requires that a female's ovum (egg) be fertilized by a male's gamete (sperm) to achieve human conception. There simply is no other option short of a miracle."[100]

What God was saying to Satan at the time of the fall was that Jesus, the Messiah, was going to arrive on planet Earth by an "unnatural" means [aka the virgin birth] and would crush his [Satan's] head! What's incredible to think about is that when Jesus went to the cross to pay our debts, Satan probably threw a party, thinking he had won. However, as prophesied by God, all that was done to Jesus was merely a bruise to the heel of the Messiah. One day, hopefully soon, the Messiah will return and crush the head of Satan, fulfilling the rest of that prophecy. *"Amen. Come, Lord Jesus!"* (Revelation 22:20c).

[100] Sean McDowell, "Is there Evidence?" *SeanMcDowell.org*.

Because Jesus was not born under the sin curse that comes through man's seed, He was born sinless. This is why the doctrine of the virgin birth is of the utmost importance and is an essential component of the Christian faith. It is the only way that Jesus could *"be born in the likeness of men"* (Philippians 2:7c), yet be *"like that of a lamb without blemish or spot"* (1 Peter 1:19b). If Jesus were not born of a virgin, He would have been born into the same sin that the rest of humanity has been subject to since the fall in the Garden of Eden. He had to be born of a virgin! There is no doubt the virgin birth of Jesus is a miracle, as so eloquently expressed here:

> *In the virgin birth, the immaterial (the Spirit) and the material (Mary's womb) were both involved . . . Only God can make something out of nothing; only God could perform the miracles of creation, the incarnation, and the virgin birth. The virgin birth is important in that it preserves the truth that Jesus is fully God and fully man at the same time. His physical body He received from Mary. But His eternal, holy nature was His from all eternity past (see John 6:69).*[101]

Given the importance of the virgin birth, it is no surprise that we have additional supporting evidence in the Gospels.

HERE'S THE TANGIBLE EVIDENCE FOR THE VIRGIN BIRTH!

The entire time that Jesus was gruesomely and brutally tortured, then nailed to a cross with giant spikes placed through His hands and feet and a piercing crown of thorns shoved into His head, one person was standing by, watching in complete agony . . . His mother, Mary! You see, IF she knew that Jesus was a product of

[101] Got Questions Editors, nd, "Why Is the Virgin Birth so Important?" *Got Questions Ministries.*

rape or unwed sex with Joseph, all she had to do was yell for them to stop beating her Son to death in one of the most inhumane ways in human history. All she had to do was admit that Jesus was not the Son of God, conceived supernaturally by the Holy Spirit, but rather the son of Joseph or someone else. Perhaps this would have put an end to the brutality. Then, she might have taken her firstborn Son home to nurture Him back to health. The problem with those ideas is that Mary did not stop the crucifixion; she couldn't! In all her pain and agony, watching her Son die so horrendously, she also knew that He WAS the prophesied Messiah who was to save the world by His undeserving death. Just like she knew when it was time to reveal His divine nature at the wedding in Cana, she also knew it was His time to become the spotless sacrifice.

I don't know of a mother in all history who would have let her son die such an excruciating death IF she KNEW the virgin birth was a lie. If we're being honest, most moms would probably go as far as to lie blatantly to stop what was happening to their son, to save him from the agonizing pain. But Mary couldn't even open her mouth and lie to save Him, for she knew how Jesus was conceived in her womb. The ONE person alive who had absolute knowledge of the virgin birth was there and chose to do nothing to stop His death. And that is because the one person who knew also knew it was unequivocally true and imperative for Him to fulfill the Scriptures by way of His mission on earth—to die for the sins of the world and be resurrected to conquer death and hell.

CHAPTER 10

HOW AND WHY DID MARY AND JOSEPH ACTUALLY TRAVEL TO BETHLEHEM? DID MARY GET TO BETHLEHEM RIGHT WHEN SHE WAS DUE?

Frank Figueroa

So many ideas have been shared throughout the centuries regarding the birth of our Savior, Jesus. Many of these concepts have made their way into our heads and hearts and have even become a part of our shared Christmas story. But are these precepts trustworthy? Are they based merely on tradition and the words of men? Or are they truly based on God's infallible, eternal Word?

Let's take Mary and Joseph's travels to Bethlehem, for instance. When did they make this journey? How did they get there? Where did they stay? Did she give birth to Jesus immediately upon her arrival? The best place to go for the answers to these questions is not the internet, the movies, the Hallmark Channel, or even a good book. The best thing we can do is go directly to the Source that documents the events for us, the Bible.

Luke 2:1–7

> *And it came to pass in those days that a decree went out from Caesar Augustus that all the world should be registered. This census first took place while Quirinius was governing Syria. So all went to be registered, everyone to his own city. Joseph also went up from Galilee, out of the city of Nazareth, into Judea, to the city of David, which is called Bethlehem, because he was of the house and lineage of David, to be registered with Mary, his betrothed wife, who was with child. So it was, that while they were there, the days were completed for her to be delivered. And she brought forth her firstborn Son, and wrapped Him in swaddling cloths, and laid Him in a manger, because there was no room for them in the inn.*

Luke, a doctor and therefore more meticulous with his details, gives us the most descriptive account in all of Scripture of Mary and Joseph's travels during the days leading up to and shortly after Jesus' birth. The Gospel of John mentions Jesus' birth focusing on His divinity, while Matthew mentions the genealogies of Jesus and some of the other facets, including angelic encounters, the travels of the magi, and their encounter with Herod. (Mark doesn't even mention a single detail about Jesus' birth.) What we have read in the first seven verses of Luke is the primary source upon which all accounts of the travels of Jesus' parents must be based.

So, what happened that first Christmas? Let's start with the first words in our passage, "It came to pass." This tells us that something was being fulfilled or performed that had been foretold in times past. For many years prior, God had told the people, using His Word, that a Savior was coming in the form of the Messiah. Consider some of the fascinating details that God foretold through the prophets:

- **He would be a human.**

Genesis 3:15

And I will put enmity between you and the woman, and between your seed and her seed; He shall bruise your head, and you shall bruise His heel.

Hebrews 2:16

For indeed He does not give aid to angels, but He does give aid to the seed of Abraham.

- **He would be a Jew, not a Gentile.**

Genesis 12:1–3

Now the LORD had said to Abram: "Get out of your country, from your family and from your father's house, to a land that I will show you. I will make you a great nation; I will bless you and make your name great; and you shall be a blessing. I will bless those who bless you, and I will curse him who curses you; and in you all the families of the earth shall be blessed.

Numbers 24:17

I see Him, but not now; I behold Him, but not near; A Star shall come out of Jacob; A Scepter shall rise out of Israel, and batter the brow of Moab, and destroy all the sons of tumult.

- **He would be from the tribe of Judah.**

Genesis 49:10

The scepter shall not depart from Judah, nor a lawgiver from between his feet, until Shiloh [102] *comes; And to Him shall be the obedience of the people.*

- **He would be from the family of David.**

2 Samuel 7:1–17

- **He would be born of a virgin.**

Isaiah 7:14

Therefore the Lord Himself will give you a sign: Behold, the virgin shall conceive and bear a Son, and shall call His name Immanuel.

- **He would be born in Bethlehem, the city of David.**

Micah 5:2

But you, Bethlehem Ephrathah, though you are little among the thousands of Judah, yet out of you shall come forth to Me the One to be Ruler in Israel, whose goings forth are from of old, from everlasting.

All of this occurred just as the Scriptures said! Also, Luke mentions that Mary and Joseph were already husband and wife. But since they did not consummate the marriage until after Jesus was born, she is called his "betrothed wife."

Matthew 1:18–25

Now the birth of Jesus Christ was as follows: After His mother Mary was betrothed to Joseph, before they came together, she was found with child of the Holy Spirit. Then Joseph her husband, being a just man, and not wanting to make her a public example,

102 Shiloh = *høly^v sûiyloœ* = the Messiah; one who brings ultimate tranquility and peace.

> *was minded to put her away secretly. But while he thought about these things, behold, an angel of the Lord appeared to him in a dream, saying, "Joseph, son of David, do not be afraid to take to you Mary your wife, for that which is conceived in her is of the Holy Spirit. And she will bring forth a Son, and you shall call His name JESUS, for He will save His people from their sins."*
>
> *So all this was done that it might be fulfilled which was spoken by the Lord through the prophet, saying: "Behold, the virgin shall be with child, and bear a Son, and they shall call His name Immanuel," which is translated, "God with us."*
>
> *Then Joseph, being aroused from sleep, did as the angel of the Lord commanded him and took to him his wife, and did not know her till she had brought forth her firstborn Son. And he called His name JESUS.*

From these passages, we can glean several important details. First, a census was taken in all the major districts. This would require Joseph (and his very pregnant wife, Mary) to journey about 80–90 miles from Nazareth to Bethlehem. So how did they do it? Many depictions have Joseph walking with Mary riding behind him on a donkey. Could this be? It is a possibility that they used an animal to help carry the burden. Some have even speculated that maybe they used a donkey to pull a cart, and Mary rode in that as it would prove more comfortable. But did they even own a donkey, let alone a cart? Remember, they were an impoverished couple, reflected through the small sacrifice (two small birds) they offered after Jesus was born (Luke 2:24). The simple answer is that we don't know because we aren't told.

Let's highlight another glaring omission that many of us have seen portrayed. While it is true that there was no room for them in the inn, notice there was no innkeeper mentioned at all. I know, I know . . . This sure puts a damper on the next church play regarding Christmas, in which the "innkeeper" always plays a small but essential role. But although there may have been an innkeeper, we have no record of anyone saying, "There's no room for you here!" so we can comfortably ditch that stereotypical character as he is not mentioned in Scripture.

WE CANNOT RELY ON THE TRADITIONS OF MEN AND CHRISTMAS DECORATIONS TO TEACH US DOCTRINES REGARDING THE COMING OF OUR SAVIOR.

Another detail we often see portrayed is that Mary makes it to Bethlehem right in the nick of time as she's having contractions and gives birth to Jesus immediately upon arrival. But we see no validation for this whatsoever in Scripture. All Luke 2:6 tells us is, "So it was, that while they were there, the days were completed for her to be delivered." So, could she have made it to the manger just before Jesus was delivered? Possibly. But she also could have arrived early and been there for a while before her due date. Or, it could have been that she gave birth to Jesus days after her due date, so she still had time to spare. After all, there is one thing we can be sure of: babies are notorious for coming into the world according to God's timetable and not according to man's. And since God did not reveal a date that Jesus was to be born, we have no idea if Mary and Joseph made it to Bethlehem with or without time to spare.

Another thing to note is that Jesus is called Mary's "firstborn Son." This implies that she had other children after Him and was not a perpetual virgin like other false teachings claim. Look at Matthew 1:24-25: "Then Joseph, being aroused from sleep, did as the angel of the Lord commanded him and took to him his wife, and did not know her till she had brought forth her firstborn Son. And he called His name JESUS." Notice that Joseph did not have relations with Mary "till" she gave birth to Jesus. This implies that after Jesus' birth, they had sexual intimacy as any married couple would. Mark 6:3 records that Jesus had half brothers and sisters: "'Is this not the carpenter, the Son of Mary, and brother of James, Joses, Judas, and Simon? And are not His sisters here with us?'" So, they were offended at Him." So clearly, Mary had other children, who were noted as Jesus' brothers and sisters.

What have we learned from all of this? We cannot use "Nativity Theology" to get our depiction of what happened during the days of Jesus' birth. What I mean by this is that we cannot rely on the traditions of men and Christmas decorations to teach us doctrines regarding the coming of our Savior, Jesus, or any other biblical idea, for that matter. We must get into the Word of God and allow it to get into us so that we might see God as He revealed Himself, even as He was coming into the world as a baby, to save us from our sins.

CHAPTER 11

WAS JESUS ACTUALLY BORN IN A STABLE? WHAT IS THE SIGNIFICANCE OF SWADDLING CLOTHES AND A MANGER AS PART OF THE NATIVITY?

Dave Glander

Until you have stood in Bethlehem to experience the lay of the land personally, many historical narratives for Christ's birth are a little hard to understand. Let's start by breaking the story down so that we can better understand what was truly happening at the time of Jesus' birth. Joseph and Mary were of very humble backgrounds, and according to the text, they were likely labeled as "poor." Luke 2:24 tells us that at the time of Jesus' official presentation at the Temple, Joseph and Mary brought either a pair of turtledoves or two young pigeons as an offering to the Lord as prescribed by the Law found in Leviticus chapter 12. For wealthy people, a year-old lamb was to be the burnt offering. Still, to ensure everyone could participate in the offering, verse 8 tells us, *"And if she cannot afford a lamb, then she shall take two turtledoves or two pigeons, one for a burnt offering and the other for a sin offering. And the priest shall make atonement for her, and she shall be clean."*

This truth also helps us better understand what happened when they arrived in Bethlehem: due to their economic status, they would not be shopping for the most incredible Airbnb®. The most likely place they would've been looking for is a place to stay with family, especially given that they went to Bethlehem at that time to be a part of the "family census" conducted by the Roman authorities. Another clue we have in determining the location of Christ's birth is again found in the Gospel of Luke. There are two Greek words for "inn," and Luke uses them in different contexts to show his understanding of both. One word, "*pandocheion*," describes a public lodging place the Romans would build, commonly found along the highways between cities where travelers would find rest. Luke mentions one of these "inns" in the parable of the Good Samaritan: "He went to him and bound up his wounds, pouring on oil and wine. Then he set him on his own animal and brought him to an inn and took care of him" (Luke 10:24). However, when Luke writes about the problem Joseph and Mary had when there was "no place for them in the inn (Luke 2:7)," he uses the Greek word "*katalymati*," which translates best to a "guest room," usually on the top floor of the house. Luke's usage of these two words lets us know that he is referring to a family's "inn," not an institutional inn.

Now that we know that Joseph and Mary weren't looking for a room at the Hilton® Inn, let's shift our focus to what the home of a family in Bethlehem looked like. Sadly, this area of Bethlehem is located in what is known as the West Bank, just outside Jerusalem. The area is currently under complete Muslim control, with a staggering 92% Muslim population and only 8% Christian population. Jews are not permitted in due to the highly-protected fence and gate system surrounding the West Bank. However, a visit to this area today still reveals what the land was like at the time of Jesus.

The entire area is still known as the shepherd's town due to the vast number of ancient sites that remain today. The city sits atop a hill with a valley that separates it from Jerusalem, where the ancient Holy Temple would have existed at that time. Priests would trek across this valley (not an easy climb) to purchase their lambs for sacrifice. It is interesting to think that due to the journey (on foot) from the Temple to Bethlehem being one that would take several hours to complete, the priests would have much quiet time to think about why they were going to make the purchase and what sins they would be asking forgiveness for. Praise God that we live in a time where all we need to do is bow our heads in reverence to the King of Kings, and we have instant access to Him—our sins have already been paid in full through the work Jesus accomplished on the cross!

A common feature throughout land of Israel are caves large enough to dwell in, or in the case of King David, to hide in (1 Samuel 24). According to the locals, hundreds of homes were built on top of a natural cave. The household patriarchs would live on the first floor, and when their children became old enough to need their own space, they would build another floor on top of the parents' floor to live in. However, as was common practice, there was always an "upper" room or floor for hospitality. When Luke said there was no room in the inn, he was referring to the upper floor of the family house. Bethlehem became overwhelmed with visitors because everyone had to go to their hometowns for the census.

Logically, if you've ever traveled with a pregnant woman by car, you know how difficult it is to make her comfortable for the journey. Now, could you imagine how much more difficult it would have been for a woman in her final stages of pregnancy to travel from Nazareth to Bethlehem on foot (or maybe by donkey; the text doesn't say which)? The average time to make that journey is just over a week. However, given their circumstances, it probably took two weeks or more. It is likely that because of the time it took them to make the journey, they were among the last to arrive, and all the rooms for guests in the family's house were already taken. This would seem to suggest that the most likely place Joseph and Mary found to stay was in the basement, where the cave would have been located.

The basement level, or cave, that the house could have been built on was the perfect place for the shepherd's flock to live. It had easy ground access to move the flock in and out, as well as having a "bird's eye view" from the first floor above the cave to ensure the flock's safety from any thieves or predators. The cave's temperature would provide year-round comfort to the flock and, in many cases, natural ventilation for sanitary purposes. Interestingly, first-century shepherds figured out that if they made a small vent shaft at the top of the cave ceiling that would come into the home's first floor, the heat from the bodies of the flocks would help warm the home in the winter. Another aspect of Joseph and Mary not finding room in the house and being put in the cave with the sheep could be that Mary was about to give birth, which produced much blood. According to Jewish law in Leviticus 12, a woman is considered unclean immediately upon childbirth. This simple fact at that time would have been a great cause for concern to the homeowner and a good reason for them to suggest that Mary be housed in the basement while delivering her child, possibly explaining why Mary would have laid Him in a manger shortly after giving birth. The Greek word for manger is "*phatnē*, " meaning a "feeding trough," which would have obviously been found where the sheep were housed.

To conclude, let's also address the question regarding swaddling clothes. The answer to this one is really very simple. According to Merriam-Webster.com, "swaddling" is derived from the word "swathe," which means to bind, wrap, or swaddle with or as if with a bandage. The idea behind swaddling a baby is that it helps the baby transition from the snuggly place of the womb to the outside world. Even in modern times, new parents are taught by nurses how to wrap their babies in a swaddling wrap. Swaddling helps babies to sleep better, prevents them from scratching themselves, and reduces the risk of SIDS (sudden infant death syndrome). In ancient times, a swaddled baby was considered safe if wrapped and watched properly. Because one of the first things Luke tells us is that Mary wrapped Jesus in swaddling clothes, we know she was immediately a loving and attentive mother. There is also the fact that the shepherds were told to look for "a baby wrapped in swaddling clothes and lying in a manger" (Luke 2:12), so Mary unconsciously gave them an exact sign to know they had found the correct baby.

The fact that Jesus may have been born in a shepherd's cave, a place where priests would come to purchase a lamb for their sacrifice, could be seen as prophetic of what Jesus would eventually accomplish by being "the Lamb of God, who takes away the sin of the world!" (John 1:29b). "He was oppressed, and he was afflicted, yet he opened not his mouth; like a lamb that is led to the slaughter, and like a sheep that before its shearers is silent, so he opened not his mouth" (Isaiah 53:7). And because of this, the Apostle John said that he "saw a Lamb, looking as if it had been slain, standing at the center of the throne, encircled by the four living creatures and the elders... the four living creatures and the twenty-four elders fell down before the Lamb... You are worthy to take the scroll and to open its seals, because you were slain, and with your blood you purchased for God persons from every tribe and language and people and nation" (Revelation 5:6a, 8a, 9). "And by that will we have been sanctified through the offering of the body of Jesus Christ once for all" (Hebrews 10:10). And this is why Jesus boldly proclaims, "I am the way, the truth, and the life. No one comes to the Father except through me" (John 14:6).

CHAPTER 12

WAS THERE REALLY A STAR OF BETHLEHEM? THE STAR OF BETHLEHEM . . . DID IT MOVE? WAS IT A COMET? WHY DID IT APPEAR AND REAPPEAR? WAS IT AN ALIGNING OF THE PLANETS?

Frank Figueroa, Jr.

When it comes to the Christmas Star, much has been written. Some have speculated, while others have penned sheer fantasy. But what was the star that led people to Jesus? Was it an aligning of the planets and thus, just a natural phenomenon? Did it just sit in the night sky, or did it actually move? Was this just a once-in-a-lifetime occurrence, or should we be prepared for this to happen again?

NATURAL OR SUPERNATURAL

Let's start by looking into what I consider the most foundational question with regards to the Star of Bethlehem, or Christmas

Star. Was it an aligning of the planets and thus, just a natural phenomenon, or was it a supernatural work of God?

Some have argued that the star was probably a comet, a gathering of planets, or a supernova. These are very problematic claims. Consider, for example, the idea that if this glowing celestial object was just a natural phenomenon, it really serves no significant purpose. Natural wonders have occurred frequently throughout the centuries. Think of how many times there has been an aligning of the planets, or how many times millions of people have gathered to watch solar and lunar eclipses. Implying that the star's appearance was a natural occurrence would seem to rule out the possibility of it being a supernatural or miraculous event, which would be problematic for many reasons.

It is here that I will interject my opinion on something. I feel that the Star of Bethlehem behaved similarly to the Shekinah glory of the Lord that led God's people in the Old Testament. How did I come up with that? Think about it . . . The star appeared and disappeared on at least two different occasions. It actually moved and led people and did not just sit in the sky on the horizon like natural stars seem to do. It also only appeared to and led people God wanted to lead, and no one else saw it. The language written about this star is very similar to how God led His people in the Old Testament. Exodus 13:21 reads, *"And the LORD went before them by day in a pillar of cloud to lead the way, and by night in a pillar of fire to give them light, to go by day and night."*

Then it is said of the Star in Matthew 2:9, *"When they heard the king, they departed; and behold, the star which they had seen in the East went before them, till it came and stood over where the young Child was."* Notice that in both instances, the leading light would appear to them and then "went before them" to get them where the Lord God wanted them to go. Such an event is extremely rare and may have been perceived as highly significant to the magi. The way the star acted, however, proved to be anything but natural. This was clearly a star, but not just an ordinary star. The miraculous existence of this star was to serve one primary purpose: to lead people to the Messiah who had come into the world at this specific time.

WHY DID IT APPEAR AND REAPPEAR?

We also know that the star appeared, disappeared, and reappeared. Matthew 2:1–4 tells us that the magi saw the star before they met Herod:

> *Now after Jesus was born in Bethlehem of Judea in the days of Herod, the king, behold, wise men from the East came to Jerusalem, saying, "Where is He who has been born King of the Jews? For we have seen His star in the East and have come to worship Him." So we know definitively that they traveled towards the star towards Jerusalem. When Herod heard about this, he too looked for the star. When Herod the king heard this, he was troubled, and all Jerusalem with him. And when he had gathered all*

> *the chief priests and scribes of the people together, he inquired of them where the Christ was to be born.*

Notice that he is looking for the place where Jesus was born by looking for the same star that the magi saw, but he doesn't see it. And since he had the greatest astronomers in the land, this would have to mean that the star disappeared or remained hidden from his and their sight. Then eventually, the magi meet face-to-face with Herod, and this exchange takes place: "Then Herod, when he had secretly called the wise men, determined from them what time the star appeared. And he sent them to Bethlehem and said, 'Go and search carefully for the young Child, and when you have found *Him,* bring back word to me, that I may come and worship Him also.'" (Matthew 2:7–8)

It is clear that Herod does not want to worship Jesus but to eliminate Him. Though he was able to determine the timing at which the Christmas Star appeared based on the testimony of the wise men, he was unable to determine the location of the Christ Child, for apparently, the Star was not visible to him. Following this conversation with the king, the wise men observed something remarkable. In Matthew 2:9–12, we read,

> *When they heard the king, they departed; and behold, the star which they had seen in the East went before them, till it came and stood over where the young Child was. When they saw the star, they rejoiced with exceedingly great joy. And when they had come into the house, they saw the young Child with Mary His mother, and fell down and worshiped Him. And when they had opened their treasures, they presented gifts to Him: gold, frankincense, and myrrh. Then, being divinely warned in a dream that they should not return to Herod, they departed for their own country another way.*

Notice some very interesting things transpire. The word "behold" used in verse 9 is translated as "Look!" in the original Greek. In today's vernacular, it would mean, "Check that out!" In other words, something came into view that wasn't there before, and it blew them away! And what is the very next thing that is mentioned? The Star! The same Star that initially appeared in the direction they were to go toward now reappears (at least to them) and starts to move by "going before them," just as the Shekinah glory did many years prior.

Where does it lead them? Not to the manger, but to a house where Jesus is. By this time, He is no longer an infant but a young child, and this is when they will present gifts to Him.[103] Some of the key points can be summarized as follows:

- The Star appears to have only been revealed to those God was leading to His Son, Jesus.
- It seems the Star may have initially acted as a sign and disappeared by the time the wise men arrived in Jerusalem (a 400–700-mile journey taking weeks or even months to traverse) before they met with Herod.
- The Star seemed to reappear and act as a guide when they began their much shorter journey from Jerusalem to Bethlehem, approximately six miles away.
- This time, when they journey toward the house that the young Child, Jesus, is in, the Star leads them where they need to go.

Obviously, this is not a naturally occurring phenomenon but rather a miracle that glorifies the Lord God—without Him, this could not have happened. Before we close this chapter, I want to mention one last thing that may help us answer some skeptics who try to deny the validity of the Word of God regarding the Star.

[103] Please refer to Chapter 5, "Did Jesus Really Have Three Wise Men Visit Him as a Baby?" to read about the events surrounding the wise men in greater depth.

Some will ask, "Why does the Bible say the star rose in the east if the wise men actually traveled west (towards Jerusalem from the east) to see where Jesus was born?" Matthew 2:2 says, *"Where is He who has been born King of the Jews? For we have seen His star in the East and have come to worship Him."* (emphasis added)

To answer this, we need to understand something about the Greek language. The text absolutely says, "They saw His star in the east." The word "East" = *anatolē* and is defined as "the place of rising," "the rising of the sun," and "the dawn or day spring." Therefore, this is not about where the Star is but about the regularity of this occurrence. Allow me to elaborate further for clarification. We would never say, "I'm going to watch the sun rising in the east," because the sun always rises in the east, which would be redundant. Nor do we say, "I'm going to see the sun setting in the west." Once again, redundant. The Scripture here can refer to one of two ideas: either the magi are referring to the fact that they see His star on the horizon consistently, or that the star first appeared in the eastern sky, then moved in a westward direction toward Bethlehem.

Scripture clearly says that the magi were from the east (Matthew 2:1) and that the Star initially shone consistently, as did other stars rising in the east. Here are a few closing points:

- The "Christmas Star" could not have been obvious, or Herod and all his people would not have missed it.
- Due to the rotation of the earth, neither a comet nor planets can "stand still" in a location for a duration of time. . . And the concept of standing still is the opposite of what the biblical account states.
- The Star actually moved when it appeared the second time and led them to Jesus, then a young child in a house. This observation would be inconsistent with ordinary stars.

- The only people we are told who saw the Star were the magi, making it a special revelation—something only God can do.

Rightly said was the refrain of the Christmas song "We Three Kings," which proclaims:

O Star of Wonder, Star of Night,
Star with Royal Beauty bright.
Westward leading, Still proceeding,
Guide us to Thy perfect Light.

May God guide us to His Son Jesus so that we too can experience the forgiveness of our sins—fulfilling the purpose for which He came.

BIBLIOGRAPHY

344, CIMRM. 1914. "Mithras rock-born, H. 0.63." Mithraeum. *Tertullian.org.* San Clemente, Rome. https://www.tertullian.org/rpearse/mithras/display.php?page=cimrm344.

AA Christmas Trees. 2021. "The Complicated History of the Christmas Tree." *AA Christmas Trees.* September 21. Accessed August 21, 2023. https://nychristmastrees.com/blogs/articles/the-complicated-history-of-the-christmas-tree.

Bock, Darrell. 1994. *Luke, BECNT.* Edited by Moises Silva. Vol. Vol. 1. Grand Rapids, MI: Baker Books.

Boeckmann, Catherine. 2023. "St. Nicholas Day Traditions, History, and More." *Almanac.* May 24. Accessed August 17, 2023. https://www.almanac.com/st-nicholas-day#:~:text=Nicholas%E2%80%94starting%20on%20the%205th,exchange%20them%20for%20small%20gifts.

Cairns, Earle E. 1996. *Christianity Through the Centuries.* Grand Rapids: Zondervan Academic.

Carlson, Jason. nd. "Why We Answer the Door When the Cultists Come Knocking." *ChristianMinistriesIntl.org.* Accessed September 5, 2023. https://www.christianministriesintl.org/why-we-answer-the-door-when-the-cultists-come-knocking/.

Carlson, Ron. nd. *What Do Jehovah's Witnesses Believe?* Accessed September 5, 2023. https://www.christianministriesintl.org/videos/CMIC5RCJW1.mp4.

Clauss, Manfred. 2001. *The Roman Cult of Mithras: The God and His Mysteries.* 1st Edition. Translated by Richard Gordon. Milton Park: Routledge.

Del Rosario, Mikel. 2013. "Did Luke Get the Christmas Story Wrong?" *Voice* (Dallas Theological Seminary). https://voice.dts.edu/article/did-luke-get-the-christmas-story-wrong-del-rosario-mikel/.

Dunker, Marilee Pierce. 2018. "The Origins of Decorating the Christmas Tree." *World Vision.* November 30. Accessed August 17, 2023. https://www.worldvision.org/christian-faith-news-stories/origins-decorating-christmas-tree#:~:text=Our%20faith%20in%20Christ%20stays,probably%20the%20first%20decorated%20tree.

Editors of Encyclopedia Brittanica. n. d. "Santa Claus." *Brittanica.* Accessed August 17, 2023. https://www.britannica.com/topic/Santa-Claus.

Emilsson, Eyjólfur. 2021. "Porphyry." *The Stanford Encyclopedia of Philosophy.* February 17. Accessed September 7, 2023. https://plato.stanford.edu/entries/porphyry/.

Ferguson, Everett. 2003. *Backgrounds of Early Christianity.* 3rd Edition. Grand Rapids, MI: Eerdmans.

Finnegan, Jack. 1959. *Light from the Ancient Past.* Princeton: Princeton University Press.

Fowler, W. Warde. 2019. *The Roman Festivals of the Period of the Republic: An Introduction to the Study of the Religion of the Romans.* Glasgow: Good Press.

Giunta, Blake. nd. "Was Horus Born of a Virgin (Isis-Mary)?" *Belief Map.* Accessed September 6, 2023. https://beliefmap.org/jesus/exist/myth-copy/horus/virgin-birth.

Got Questions Ministries. nd. "Should We Have a Christmas Tree?" *Got Questions Ministries.* Accessed August 17, 2023. https://www.gotquestions.org/Christmas-tree.html.

—. nd. "What Are the Jehovah's Witnesses' Beliefs About Jesus' Return in 1914?" *GotQuestions.Org.* Accessed September 5, 2023. https://www.gotquestions.org/Jehovahs-Witnesses-1914.html.

—. nd. "What Does It Mean to Come Out From Among Them?" *GotQuestions.org.* Accessed September 5, 2023. https://www.gotquestions.org/come-out-from-among-them.html.

—. nd. "What Does the Bible Say About Traditionalism?" *Got Questions Ministries.* Accessed August 18, 2023. https://www.gotquestions.org/traditionalism.html.

—. nd. "Why Is the Virgin Birth so Important?" *Got Questions Ministries.* Accessed September 8, 2023. https://www.gotquestions.org/virgin-birth.html.

Green Global Travel. 2022. "History & 25 Other Names for Santa Claus Around the World (with 55 Fun Facts!)." *Green Global Travel.* December 2. Accessed August 7, 2023. https://greenglobaltravel.com/other-names-for-santa-claus-around-the-world/.

Hillibish, Jim. 2008. "The Evolution of Santa: From Nasty to Nice and Everything in Between." *The State Journal-Register.* December 21. Accessed August 17, 2023. https://www.sj-r.com/story/news/2008/12/21/the-evolution-santa-from-nasty/47934244007/.

History.com Editors. 2023. "History of Christmas Trees." *History.* April 24. Accessed August 17, 2023. https://www.history.com/topics/christmas/history-of-christmas-trees#how-did-christmas-trees-start.

—. 2023. "Santa Claus." *History.* April 20. Accessed August 17, 2023. https://www.history.com/topics/christmas/santa-claus.

Hond, Paul. 2021. "The Story Behind the Most Famous Christmas Poem of All." *Columbia Magazine.* November 19. Accessed August 17, 2023. https://magazine.columbia.edu/article/story-behind-most-famous-christmas-poem-all.

Jasiński, Jakub. n.d. "Dies Natalis Solis Invicti." *IMPERIUM ROMANUM.* Accessed June 11, 2023. https://imperiumromanum.pl/en/roman-religion/roman-feasts/dies-natalis-solis-invicti/.

Jehovah's Witnesses. n.d. "Why Don't Jehovah."

Josephus, Flavius. 1895. *The Works of Flavius Josephus.* Translated by A.M. William Whiston. Auburn and Buffalo: John E. Beardsley.

Kavon, Eli. 2017. "Emperor Julian and the Dream of a Third Temple." *The Jerusalem Post*, December 4. Accessed September 8, 2023. https://www.jpost.com/opinion/emperor-julian-and-the-dream-of-a-third-temple-516999.

Largen, Kristin Johnston. 2011. *Baby Krishna, Infant Christ: A Comparative Theology of Salvation.* Maryknoll, NY: Orbis Books.

Mark, Joshua J. 2016. "Horus." *World History Encyclopedia.* March 16. Accessed September 8, 2023. https://www.worldhistory.org/Horus/.

Massey, Gerald. 1994. *Egyptian Book of the Dead and the Ancient Mysteries of Amenta.* Buffalo: EWorld, Inc.

Matson, Cindy. 2023. "Let's Turn Pride Month in to Prayer Month." *Bible Study Nerd (blog).* May 30. Accessed June 11, 2023. https://biblestudynerd.home.blog/2023/05/30/lets-turn-pride-month-into-prayer-month/.

McDaniel, Spencer. 2019. "Was Jesus copied Off the Egyptian God Horus?" *Tales of Times Forgotten.* November 24. Accessed September 8, 2023.

https://talesoftimesforgotten.com/2019/11/24/was-jesus-copied-off-the-egyptian-god-horus/.

McDowell, Josh and McDowell, Sean. 1999. *The New Evidence That Demands a Verdict.* Nashville: Thomas Nelson.

McDowell, Sean. 2017. "Is There Evidence Jesus Was Born of a Virgin?" *SeanMcDowell.org.* December 23. Accessed September 8, 2023. https://seanmcdowell.org/blog/is-there-evidence-jesus-was-born-of-a-virgin.

Miles, Clement A. 2021. *Christmas in Ritual and Tradition, Christian and Pagan.* Indo-European Publishing.

Murdock, D. M. 2009. *Christ in Egypt: The Horus-Jesus Connection.* Ashland,, OR: Stellar House Publishers. https://www.google.com/books/edition/Christ_in_Egypt/Iaqe9CG_s6cC?hl=en&gbpv=1&dq=Isis+%26+"perpetual+virgin"&pg=PA153&printsec=frontcover.

Nissenbaum, Stephen. 1997. *The Battle for Christmas: A Cultural History of America's Most Cherished Holiday.* New York: Vintage.

Orr, James. 1907. *The Virgin Birth of Christ.* New York: Charles Scribner's Sons.

Oswalt, John N. 2009. *The Bible Among the Myths: Unique Revelation or Just Ancient Literature?* Grand Rapids, MI: Zondervan Academic.

Patrick Young, Esq. 2017. "How German Refugee Thomas Nast Invented How Santa Claus Looks Back During the Civil War." *Long Island Wins.* December 18. Accessed August 17, 2023. https://longislandwins.com/es/columns/immigrants-civil-war/german-refugee-thomas-nast-invented-santa-claus-looks-civil-war/.

Pearce, Tony. n.d. "Messiah to be Descended from David." *The Messiah Factor.* https://messiahfactor.com/messiah-to-be-descended-from-david/.

Porphyry. nd. "On Images, Fragment 7." *The Internet Classics Archive.* Accessed September 7, 2023. http://classics.mit.edu/Porphyry/images.html.

Puku'i, Mary. n. d. "Kana Koloka." *Huapala.org.* Accessed August 17, 2023. https://www.huapala.org/ChristReligious/Kana_Kaloka.html.

Ramsay, William. 1898. *Was Christ Born in Bethlehem?* London: Hodder and Stoughton.

Rhodes, John H. 2011. "Josephus Misdated the Census of Quirinius." *Journal of the Evangelical Theological Society*, March: 65-87.

Rice, John R. 1955. *The King of the Jews: A Commentary on the Gospel According to Matthew.* Grand Rapids, MI: Zondervan.

Sacred-texts.com. nd. "VIII. The Legend of the Death and Resurrection of Horus, and Other Magical Texts." *Sacred-texts.com.* Accessed September 7, 2023. https://www.sacred-texts.com/egy/leg/leg11.htm.

Samosata, Lucian of. 2009. *Works of Lucian of Samosata.* Alexandria: Library of Alexandria.

Scott, Bruce. 2006. "Herod the Not-So-Great." *Israel My Glory*, November/December. https://israelmyglory.org/article/herod-the-not-so-great/.

Sheler, Jeffrey. 1999. *Is the Bible True?* New York: HaperSanFrancisco/Zondervan.

Shelley, Bruce L. 1999. "Is Christmas Pagan?" *Christianity Today*, December 6: 85.

Sherwin-White, A. N. 1963. *Roman Society and Roman Law in the New Testament.* Oxford: Clarendon Press.

2007. *Zeitgeist: The Series.* Directed by Peter Joseph. Performed by Sideways-Film. https://www.sidewaysfilm.com/zeitgeist-the-series/.

St. Nicholas Center. n. d. "The Evil Butcher." *St. Nicholas Center.* Accessed August 17, 2023. https://www.stnicholascenter.org/who-is-st-nicholas/stories-legends/traditional-stories/early-miracles/evil-innkeeper.

Strobel, Lee. 2005. *The Case for Christmas.* Grand Rapids, MI: Zondervan.

—. 2013. "Was the resurrection of Jesus a story taken from mythology?" *Bible Gateway Blog.* April 4. Accessed September 8, 2023. https://www.biblegateway.com/blog/2013/04/bible-qa-was-jesus-resurrection-stolen-from-mythology/.

Surviving Paradise. 2022. *"Why Don't Jehovah's Witnesses Celebrate Christmas?* December 26. Accessed September 5, 2023. https://www.youtube.com/watch?v=vwmYGIyx0Ak&t=131s.

Tertullian. nd. "Mithras and Christianity." *Tertullian.org.* Accessed September 8, 2023. https://www.tertullian.org/rpearse/mithras/display.php?page=mithras_and_christianity.

The Archaeologist Editor Group. 2021. "Saint Nicholas of Myra: The Real Story Behind Santa Claus." *The Archaelogist.* December 6. Accessed

August 17, 2023. https://www.thearchaeologist.org/blog/saint-nicholas-of-myra-the-real-story-behind-santa-claus.

The Editors of Encyclopaedia Britannica. 2023. "St. Nicholas Day." *Britannica.* July 28. Accessed August 17, 2023. https://www.britannica.com/topic/Saint-Nicholas-Day.

Watchtower Bible and Tract Society. nd. "1904 Zion's Watch Tower." *Archive.org.* Accessed September 5, 2023. https://archive.org/details/1904ZionsWatchTower/page/n689/mode/2up.

—. 1921. "1921 The Golden Age Magazine." *Archive.org.* Accessed September 5, 2023. https://archive.org/details/1921TheGoldenAgeMagazine/page/n745/mode/2up.

—. nd. "The King Refines His People Spiritually." *JW.ORG.* Accessed September 5, 2023. https://wol.jw.org/en/wol/d/r1/lp-e/1102014249.

Watchtower Society. nd. "Who Is the Archangel Michael?" *JW.ORG.* Accessed September 5, 2023. https://www.jw.org/en/bible-teachings/questions/archangel-michael/.

—. nd. "Why Don't Jehovah's Witnesses Celebrate Christmas?" *JW.ORG.* Accessed September 5, 2023. https://www.jw.org/en/jehovahs-witnesses/faq/why-not-celebrate-christmas/.

ABOUT THE AUTHORS/EDITORS

CARL KERBY,
CONTRIBUTING WRITER & EDITOR

As President and Co-Founder of Reasons for Hope* Inc., Carl's passion is to train and equip the next generation to be able to stand boldly on the Word of God. He received Jesus Christ as his Lord and Savior on May 15, 1987; two years later, he was introduced to the importance of biblical authority at a Back to Genesis Conference. This experience made such an impact on him that for the next six years, he volunteered at these conferences across the globe. In 1993, Carl was invited to serve on the Board of Directors for Answers in Genesis (AiG). Ten years later, he joined AiG as a full-time speaker and Vice President for Ministry Relations. Starting in 2010, the Lord burdened Carl to focus solely on reaching the younger generation. To accomplish this calling, he left AiG and co-created Reasons for Hope* Inc. (RforH) in January 2011.

Carl has been married to his wife, Masami, for over 40 years. They live in Northern Kentucky and enjoy time spent with their two children, five grandchildren, and a beagle pup named Snoopy Deux.

FRANK FIGUEROA, JR.,
CONTRIBUTING WRITER

Frank is currently pastoring a church in Hawaii and has been thrilled to serve alongside Carl Kerby and the rest of the RforH team as a speaker. As a teenager, Frank had an ambition to be a rock star, but a friend invited him to a Bible study in the fall of 1985, and there he found himself being confronted by the authority of

God's Word. Within five minutes, Frank's life was never the same. His education includes a degree in science education, as well as studies in theology and music. He and his wife, April, love serving together and, out of their interest in bow-hunting, formed Centershot Hawaii, an archery ministry to reach out to the children in their community. This outreach has taken them as far as American Samoa and Romania! It is through God's grace and mercy that Frank can share the good news of God's Son, Jesus, with as many people as He will allow...To Him be all honor, glory, and praise, now and forever more.

DAVE GLANDER, CONTRIBUTING WRITER

Dave joined RforH in 2021 where he serves as a speaker and writer, as well as the leader of our Mic'd Up ministry. His story began in a strongly non-Christian environment where he naturally became a devout atheist. When he was thirty years old, he was on the brink of suicide and desperately cried out to a God whom he didn't even believe existed. It was at this moment that Dave was dramatically changed and filled with inexplicable peace. He had no choice but to accept the fact that a supernatural God must exist after all. He began to study various world religions, found them lacking, and was given the book *A Case for Christ*, which included the information he was seeking. Not only did he acknowledge Jesus as the One true God and his personal Savior, but he was also introduced to the discipline of apologetics. He is now a deeply committed believer in Jesus Christ and the Bible.

Dave also founded EQUIP Retreat, an apologetics summer camp training students with absolute truth to support their Christian faith, empowering them to own their faith, and challenging them to develop the boldness to share it with others. He has also taught at national and regional conferences, universities, churches, and youth camps around the country.

Dave currently lives in the Atlanta area with his wife, Stephanie, and is the proud parent of Marc, who is married to Alyssa.

DAVID MADSEN, CONTRIBUTING WRITER

David is a professor of English at Maranatha Baptist University, where he teaches composition and literature and has presented workshops on biblical worldview. His training includes a bachelor's degree in Bible from Moody Bible Institute and a master's degree in English from Liberty University, and he has taught for over twenty years on the high school and college levels. He has contributed to Reasons for Hope's Apologetics broadcasts as a scriptwriter and has written for a variety of other publications. He team-teaches a teen Sunday School class at his local church and serves as chaplain for a local factory.

David and his wife, Melissa, have been married since 1997 and have four daughters. They live in southern Wisconsin.

CANDACE NORDINE, CONTRIBUTING WRITER

Candace is the Communications Manager and "Knower of All Stuff" at RforH. She grew up as a PK (pastor's kid), and though she had a knowledge of who God was from a very young age, it wasn't until her middle school years that she truly made her faith her own. Serving in full-time ministry for the past two decades, Candace understands the need for the next generation to have biblical answers that will help equip them to stand boldly on the Word of God.

Candace is a wife, mom, teacher, employee, cook, interior decorator, designer, etc., but her greatest role is being a daughter of the King. She is thankful that God uses ordinary people just like her (1 Corinthians 1:26–31). She currently lives in northern Kentucky with her amazing husband and four very cool daughters who keep her young and hip.

ANDY STEARNS,
CONTRIBUTING WRITER

Andy currently serves as an assistant professor at Faith Baptist Bible College and as part of the adjunct faculty at Faith Baptist Theological Seminary in Ankeny, Iowa. He received his B.S. at Faith Baptist Bible College and his M.A. and M.Div. degrees at Faith Baptist Theological Seminary; he also holds a master's in theology from Central Baptist Theological Seminary. He enjoys studying theology, apologetics, and keeping up with the latest technology. Andy is also a co-creator of The Thinklings Podcast, a weekly podcast that talks about books, ministry, and always a passage from the Scriptures. The goal is to learn to renew the mind rather than entertain it with aimless scrolling through social media.

When he's not teaching, Andy enjoys pursuing the perfect cup of coffee, and may, at times, take coffee a little too seriously. Andy has been married to his amazing wife, Robyn, since 2001 and loves spending time with her and their two energetic kids.

HOLLY VARNUM,
REASONS FOR HOPE EDITOR & PROOFREADER

Holly serves as our Director of Curriculum Development, blog manager, and speaker. With degrees in education, curriculum and instruction, and educational administration, Holly has decades of experience in working with teens and adults in camp ministry, teaching and administration, and curriculum writing (A Beka Book, Focus on the Family, and Answers in Genesis, to name a few). Saved at a very young age and serving the Lord ever since, she has a passion for God's truth and communicating it with others. She is so thankful God has provided her with a well-rounded perspective through service as a classroom teacher, instructional coach, administrator, camp counselor, Sunday School teacher, ladies' Bible Study teacher, and conference speaker.

Along with her husband, Paul, she enjoys any time they can spend with their three grown daughters, two sons-in-law, and four grandchildren (so far!). She lives between the beautiful states of Maine and southern New Jersey, and yes, eats lobster (properly pronounced "lobstah") whenever she gets a chance!

JUAN VALDES,
THEOLOGY REVIEWER & EDITOR

Juan is the Senior Pastor of a Spanish-speaking congregation and a senior speaker and writer with RforH. He has a passion for youth and apologetics and has worked with young people for many years as a Christian middle and high school Chaplain and teacher of Bible and Introduction to Philosophy. His love for learning and teaching led to graduate work at Trinity Evangelical Divinity School, as well as master's degrees from both Liberty Baptist Theological Seminary and Logos Graduate School. He also holds a Doctor of Ministry degree in Apologetics from Southern Evangelical Seminary. Juan has taught theology, Bible, and apologetics at the seminary level in *both* English and Spanish and is an influential promoter of apologetics in the greater Miami area. He speaks regularly across the country and internationally at pastor's conferences, youth conferences, summer camps, apologetics conferences, and local church events.

Juan and his wife Daisy have been married for 34 years and have two college-age kids, Juan Elias, and Jessica. Together they serve in multiple areas of ministry in Miami, Florida.

DAN LIETHA,
ILLUSTRATOR

Dan joined RforH in 2019 as our cartoonist and illustrator, developing images and speaker slides that challenge viewers to think biblically. "Truth Jabs" is his newest cartoon feature, and he also produces an online educational video series called "Draw It & Know It!" instructing viewers on how to draw animals and think about them with a biblical worldview. Dan was impacted at a very young age by two things that dramatically directed the course of his life ... receiving Jesus Christ as his Lord and Savior and drawing! After high school, he attended and graduated from the Joe Kubert School of Cartoon and Graphic Art in 1987. Three years later, a biblical creation video series titled "Understanding Genesis" began a growing hunger in Dan to learn about biblical creation and the foundations of the Christian faith. One message in that video series inspired Dan to develop a comic strip called "CreationWise." Eventually, that comic strip led Dan to volunteer for (and later work for) the ministry that became Answers in Genesis as full-time cartoonist and illustrator.

Dan loves camp ministry and has spoken at camps and other venues over the past 15 years. He lives in northern Kentucky with his wife, Marcia, and daughter, Hannah.

HANNAH DUKES,
EDITOR & PROOFREADER

Hannah currently volunteers as an editor, proofreader, and writer for RforH. She has always been fascinated with words, so the opportunity to preview and edit this book has been a combination of this love of words with her love of the truth of Jesus Christ and the way His truth affects every part of our lives. It has been an honor to come alongside the authors of these articles and be blessed, impacted, and challenged by what they share. Her prayer is that God would use this book in mighty ways to impact the next generation! She is very happily married to her husband, Shannon, and homeschools their two children.

Milton Keynes UK
Ingram Content Group UK Ltd.
UKHW020929231123
433129UK00016B/889